CR

own posters to

ration and innovation on this mountain.

After interviewing over 300 people for this mountain memoir, I found great joy in the opinions of some old timers who consider the newcomers, the snowboarders who flip and fly, "a miserable bunch of buzzards." My joy came in the knowledge that at one time, the old timers were equally rabid ski fanatics. Everett Darr wrote in the 1936 *Wy'east Climbers' Annual*:

"The deep timberline snows bury the glade 20 to 30 feet. We ski over the (cabin) roof and zoom into the air on the lower side," not so unlike those buzzards of today.

With that joy comes sadness at lost voices. There are so many.

On November 14, 1997, I telephoned Carl Reynolds who bought Multorpor in 1950 and Ski Bowl in 1964. His son Chuck answered. He told me that his father had died two days earlier. "Carl would have loved your book project," he told me. So instead of an interview, Carl's hand-screened print of Ski Bowl adorns this text.

Why do I write, someone asked me recently. The answer is easy: it's like shouting "single" while in lift line. I make a new ski friend whether I am riding an old Riblet double or I am interviewing skiers and writing of rope tows, moguls and skiing the Glade. ▽

Last Tracks

On June 23, 1997, 85-year-old Hank Lewis strapped a trash barrel to his back. He hiked to a wildflower-filled meadow to haul out burned debris from the Wy'east Climbers' hut. The U.S. Forest Service torched the old cabin which of late had fallen victim to sun and wind, ice and snow.

I was a year into writing this book before I realized what a momentous effort it took for Hank to participate in the burning of his beloved Wy'east cab-in there on the southern flank of Mt. Hood. Most of the early Wy'east members were gone: Ray Atkeson, Ole Lien, Joe Leuthold and others.

The burned cabin completed a changing of the guard from the veteran mountaineers who set the pace for climbing, skiing and ski patrolling to the ski-business professionals and their adventurous skiing and snowboarding guests.

The young professionals, Jeff Kohnstamm at Timberline, Kirk Hanna at Ski Bowl, Dave Riley at Mt. Hood Meadows, and Charlie Wessinger at Summit Ski Area ride winter sports into the millennium in an oft repeated cycle of inspi-

The Oregon Winter Sports Association promoted skiing on Oregon's slopes. "To decide the Winter Sports Carnival court, we sold pins,' recalls Helen Mills Stoll, court runner-up in 1940. "The girls who sold the most pins at 10 cents each were on the court. The group took us to civic clubs where we danced and sang to promote skiing at Timberline and the whole mountain."

TIMBERLINE

and A Century of Skiing on Mt. Hood

JEAN ARTHUR

Featuring Photography by Ray Atkeson and Hugh Ackroyd

WHITEFISH EDITIONS

1792	Mt. Hood named for Lord Samuel Hood
1805	Lewis & Clark expedition travels past Mt. Hood on the Columbia River.
1849	U.S. government sends troops west to establish posts along the Oregon Trail. Troops camp near what's now known as Government Camp.
1890	Langille brothers ski on Mt. Hood's north side.
1922	U.S. Highway 26 paved.
1926	USFS draws up first plans for south-slope lodge. U.S. Highway 26 plowed for winter access.
1927	Summit ski slope and toboggan run opens. Swim jump hill opens.
1928	Multorpor jump hill opens.
1931	Harold Hirsch/White Stag sews America's first ski clothing.
1935-1936	Summit builds rope tow.
1936	Sun Valley builds the world's first chairlift. First Golden Rose Race.
1936-1937	Emilio Pucci coaches Reed Ski Team. Timberline Lodge constructed. Davidson builds "Snow Kitty," the first over-the-snow machine for ski area use.
1937	President Roosevelt dedicates Timberline Lodge. Sir Arnold Lunn opens his namesake race at Timberline. Hjalmar Hvam invents world's first workable safety release binding. Ski Bowl installs rope tow. Wy East Climbers and Nile River Yacht Club ask USFS for a ski patrol.
1938	Timberline Lodge opens for business. Mt. Hood Ski Patrol forms with 50 members.
1939	Mazama club builds rope tow and installs lights for night skiing on Mazama Hill. Magic Mile chairlift opens as one of America's first chairlifts. U.S. National Amateur and Open Downhill and Slalom Ski Championships held at Timberline and Ski Bowl.
1940s	Stormy Petrels form as possibly the world's first all-women ski patrol.
1942-1945	Timberline closed during World War II.
1949	New paved road to Timberline completed. Mt. Hood Ski Patrol's Howard Johnson invents Johnson Splint.
1951	Skiway opens as America's second tramway.
1955	R.L. Kohnstamm leases Timberline from USFS. Ski Bowl builds double chair.
1956	Timberline opens first Summer Racing Camp. Timberline builds Pucci double chairlift.
1958	Mt. Hood Ski Patrol imports a new toboggan, the akia. Timberline builds a swimming pool which opens in 1959.
1961	Portland Jaycees organize America's first Amputee Ski School.
1962	Timberline opens new Magic Mile double chairlift.
1964	Ski Bowl joins Multorpor to form one ski area.
1966	Timberline opens Victoria Station chairlift. Everett Darr builds T-bar at Summit.
1967	Multorpor installs lights for night skiing. First Nordic Ski School opens.
1968	Mt. Hood Meadows opens with 2 chairlifts and 5 runs. U.S. Highway 35 around the mountain completed for winter use.
1972	National Register of Historic Places lists Timberline Lodge on registry.
1979	Timberline opens Palmer chairlift for summer skiing.
1981	Timberline opens Blossom lift. Wy'east Day Lodge opens at Timberline.
1984	Bill Johnson wins the Olympic Gold Downhill race. Sarajevo.
1988	Friends of Silcox begin restoration of Silcox Hut. Mountain Locater Units available for mountain climbers on Mt. Hood.
1990	High Cascade Snowboard Camp builds Timberline's first half pipe.
1992	Timberline replaces Magic Mile double chair with Express quad.
1997	Timberline replaces Palmer double chair with Express quad.

Whitefish Editions

Whitefish, Montana

First edition published 1998

Copyright © Jean Arthur, 1998

Library of Congress Catalog Card Number: 98-89155

ISBN 0-9645477-0-8

10 9 8 7 6 5 4 3 2 1

Printed in the United States of America
Book design by Diane Hokans
Front cover photo of Timberline Lodge © Ray Atkeson Image Archive 1945
Back cover photo of Mt. Hood Sunset © Jean Arthur 1998
Matchbooks courtesy Jon Tullis
Placemat art of Mt. Hood recreation area from 1940 courtesy Darr Collection

About the Author

Jean Arthur was born and raised under the early morning shadow of Mt. Hood. She first skied as a four-year-old on A&T skis and leather boots.

"My earliest ski memory is of the rope tow rather than actually skiing. I'd grip the icy rope on Multorpor's bunny hill, get part way up the slope, and then slide backwards into the next kid while the rope slipped through my mittens."

Arthur grew up in Boring, attended Sam Barlow High School, graduated from the University of Oregon's Journalism School and received a Master of Fine Arts degree in Creative Writing from the University of Montana.

During Jean's undergraduate years, Timberline's Ticket Office Manager, Linda Reid hired her, "because I could read her handwriting."

Her first book, *Hellroaring: Fifty Years on The Big Mountain*, published in 1996, received national recognition in *Ski* magazine and other publications. In 1998, the

ARTHUR PHOTO

Jean Arthur

International Skiing History Association honored her with the Skade Award for excellence in regional history preservation.

She lives with her husband, Lynn Sellegren, and their children Eric, Gretchen and Bridger, in Whitefish, Montana.

INTRODUCTION

Sitzmarks and Remarks

Like millions of school kids, I grew up with the image of Timberline's Magic Mile chairlift etched on to my school folder and into my daydreams. The "Pee-Chee" sketch showed a woman riding the single-seater chair. The 1948 photograph is by *Life* magazine photographer Ralph Crane of skier Merrie Douna.

Just as the Pee-Chee introduced many youngsters to the ski scene, it introduces each chapter in this reminiscence.

I have always felt that Mt. Hood is my private playground.

I learned to ski on its slopes as a four-year-old, and often felt its pull on a rare sunny day in winter when friends and I skipped school to ski. I felt its unfading beauty one memorable spring evening when the setting sun colored the rising full moon a Pee-Chee gold. I met many a life-long friend on this mountain, and

16-021 Timberline Lodge in Mid-Winter

"The rotary snow plows used to blow snow out of the parking lot and cars were nearly buried," says Hank Lewis, who perches on top of Timberline Lodge in 1938. Tom Terry skis down the roof. Timberline Lodge is located in the Mt. Hood National Forest.

Pee-Chee® girl Merrie Douna's image graces the Mead Corporation's school folder. The drawing is from a photograph by Ralph Crane that appeared in *Life* magazine in 1948.

consider the mountain itself as one of those friends. I know others feel the same attraction to Mt. Hood.

Some of the mountain's friends no longer climb and ski, yet they left a legacy of adventure, innovation, education and competition.

The snow and cold inspired Portland skier Harold Hirsch to design America's first ski clothing: White Stag.

A couple of broken bones provoked Hjalmar Hvam to create the first safety binding.

When chairlifts first appeared in North America, Timberline became America's first ski area to build a ski lift with steel towers. Now Timberline is North America's only year-round ski resort.

I've always wanted to ski off the roof of Timberline Lodge like ski patroller Hank Lewis and Portlander Tom Terry did some 50 years ago. I've always wanted to do a flip on skis into the Timberline pool with ski instructor Doug Kinne. Since I'll accomplish neither, I'll simply take my hat off in gratitude and awe to the skiers and snowboarders who have made a century on Mt. Hood truly remarkable.

Thanks

This book would not have been possible without the enthusiasm, recollections and research support of Richard L. Kohnstamm. His good humor, historic interests and ski knowledge are interwoven throughout this text.

Mt. Hood skiers have a proud tradition of generosity from free ski schools to volunteer labor to build clubhouses and ski jumps. In following that tradition, skiers generously offered their stories, photos and memorabilia for this publication. I thank them for sharing their memories.

Additionally, I thank those writers who came before me and for whose work I have great respect. Among the hundreds of published news clippings, magazines articles and books that I consulted for this publication, the following were the most helpful: *McNeil's Mount Hood* by Fred McNeil; *Mount Hood: A Com-*

Gelandesprung

plete History by Jack Grauer; *A Pictorial History of Downhill Skiing* by Stan Cohen; and *Timberline Lodge: A Love Story* edited by Judith Rose. Both the Multnomah and Hood River County Libraries offer over a century of newspapers from the state, including the *Oregonian*, the *Oregon Journal* and the *Hood River Glacier*. The Friends of Timberline have an extensive library of Mt. Hood and Timberline artifacts.

Finally, I would like to thank my dad, Gerald E. Arthur, for teaching me to ski. I dedicate this book to him.

To live and not ski is a sad life…
But to ski …
this is to be alive!

— Hjalmar Hvam

**Opposite page:
A skier ascends
Mt. Hood's south
flank during a
sunrise climb,
pre-World War II.**

With over a century of old hickories under their feet, Northwesterners remain enamored with sliding over snow. Living in the shadow of the Cascade Mountain Range, Oregonians and Washingtonians endure steam and ash pumping from the Cascade's throttles. They tolerate the drip and dry years, and they eagerly await the snow that ices their volcanoes 30 feet thick.

Annually, over three million skier and snowboarder visits slice tracks across the Cascade's 18 ski areas and resorts. The scope of skiing's impact on Oregon reaches $160 million annually, according to the Oregon Snowsport Industries Association. The seven-billion-dollar American ski industry has roots in Northern Europe and the Alps. Yet ski equipment and ski implements experienced a fast-paced evolution this century in the Pacific Northwest, a revolution that rides the cusp into the next century.

Norwegians created skiing for sport. Brits popularized ski holidays. New Englanders and Californians engaged the public's attention to racing. But it was the West's brash individualism, intense weather and vast mountain ranges that inspired some of skiing's most innovative breakthroughs in ski patrolling, instruction, ski equipment and ski area machinery.

SPEICHER COLLECTION

Harper's Weekly: A Journal of Civilization featured "Skee-running on the Snow-covered Hills of Oregon" for the cover of the March 4, 1899, issue. While visiting Oregon's Blue Mountains, artist W.A. Rogers noted that "a clever device used in walking on skees is a round wooden block, like a little wheel, slipped over the lower end of the balance-pole, to prevent the pole from sinking down when thrust into the soft snow."

The recorded skiing history of Mt. Hood begins over a century ago during one of Mt. Hood's harshest winters. Cloud Cap Inn opened on the northern slopes in 1889 at the 5,837-foot level. It was feared that snow had crushed the hostelry. Two Hood River Valley brothers skied to Cloud Cap to check on the hut.

In his book *Wy'east The Mountain*, Fred McNeil writes: "Will and H.D. Langille, on home-made skis, set out for a visit in February (1890). ... The building was unharmed. This was the first skiing trip on record to the north side of Mount Hood."

Skiing soon traversed from mountains to magazine covers, articles to advertising. "Skee-running in Oregon" appeared in the March 4, 1899, issue of *Harper's Weekly* about skiing the Blue Mountains of Eastern Oregon.

"... (T)he inhabitants, when they wish to renew their supply of bacon and flour at the stores...put on their skees and skim over the drifts regardless of roads or beaten trails. ... I found that many people — women, men, and children were adept in the use of the skee, which is as necessary a foot-gear as a pair of arctics."

Portlanders formed the Snow Shoe Club in 1904. Members built a cabin near Cloud Cap in 1910. Likely they chose the north side of Hood because the road skirting the Columbia River remained open year-round. (U.S. Highway 26 to the mountain's southern slopes was not paved until 1922 and not plowed until 1926.)

In 1907, R.L. Glisan wrote in the *Hood River Glacier* newspaper, "In a snowstorm Friday morning, January 18, the Snow Shoe Club took the train at Union depot for Hood River on its fourth annual visit to Cloud Cap Inn, Mount Hood."

Twelve-foot-long skis were called "snow shoes," "skeys, " or "skees" (pronounced "shees") or even called "Norwegians." Snow Shoe Club members used web-footed snowshoes for the climb, and "Skees imported from Norway," for the trip down. "Improved methods of fastening snowshoes and skis were discussed, to be cussed later on.

"(Our skis knew) leaps of 100 feet," exaggerated Glisan. "The steepest grade came first and five minutes after leaving, the road resembled a battlefield. However, after many ups and downs, we caught on figuratively, having caught onto everything else en route and about an hour later 13 visions of grace somewhat bedraggled, overloaded with snow and enthusiasm, glided up to the sleighs and all aboard the horses did the rest."

South side winter recreation began in about 1900. A U.S. Forest Service (USFS) ranger used skis to travel Summit Prairie according to McNeil. A 1903 Mazama club expedition on 10-foot skis tested the perils of winter and found the skiing, "a good comparison to flying."

A few climbers utilized the 1916 Timberline Cabin, yet it wasn't until the late 1920s that "yumpers," Norwegian ski jumpers drew spectators to watch the daredevils deliver elegance and glamour to the sport.

The first winter Olympics in 1924 in Chamonix, France featured jumping and cross-country racing. Norway garnered most of the medals. Norwegian immigrants influenced skiing in the Northwest. They jumped, taught others to ski, tinkered with new ski devices, and some opened their own ski areas.

Drawn to winter like a compass needle toward the North Pole, the jumpers mesmerized hundreds of spectators at weekend jump meets in the mountain village of Government Camp. A busy weekend filled Government Camp with 800 automobiles.

The Ad Club of Portland opened Summit in 1927 with a toboggan run and ski slope. A jump hill at Swim, about a mile east of Multorpor opened that same year. Multorpor's jump hill opened in 1928, and skiers hiked up Ski Bowl during that era as well.

The Snow Shoe Club of Portland organized in 1904 as an outdoor club. Members snowshoed and skied up to Cloud Cap Chalet and other Mt. Hood areas. By 1909, the USFS estimated that 10,000 visitors camped, hiked and fished in the Mt. Hood area each year, a figure that reached 210,000 within a decade.

In 1927, Vera Nelson skied with her father, Al. She became an early member of the Cascade Ski Club, tried ski jumping off Multorpor's class "B" jump and encouraged newcomers to try ski sport.

USFS Ranger Ralph Weise soon recorded nearly 90,000 skier visits a winter. One of those skiers was Marianne Hill. She was one of only three children growing up in Government Camp, an unincorporated town named for a mid-1800s government encampment.

"I skied with Hjalmar Hvam and that group of ski jumpers," recalls Hill. "We'd hike up Ski Bowl. I skied because there was not much of anything else for a child to do in Government Camp."

Climbing was a precursor skiing, jumping and racing.

"To show you how good we were at skiing in those days," says Portlander Hank Lewis, "it took us longer to ski down from the timberline than to walk up. Nobody knew how to ski."

Mechanized tows along with the widely publicized 1932 Lake Placid Winter Olympics rode a great wave in skiing's popularity. Already, 30,000 skiers laced tracks across North American mountains according to the *Encyclopedia of Skiing*.

The introduction of the rope tow to America in 1934, allowed skiers the luxury of several runs a day. By the late 1930s, skiers were treated to rope tows at Summit, Ski Bowl and Mazama Hill. The Mazamas, an outdoor club, lit their slope for night skiing, one of the first night-skiing hills in the country.

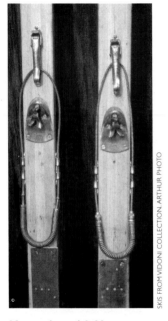

Hvooming with Hvam. Hjamer Hvam invented the world's first releasable binding and was awarded U.S. patent 2236874. He sold over 15,000 of his safety bindings.

SKIS FROM VIDONI COLLECTION. ARTHUR PHOTO

Champion ski jumper John Elvrum came to the Pacific Northwest's logging camps from Norway in 1930. He held the U.S. national amateur jumping record of 240 feet. He later built California's Snow Valley ski area.

ELVRUM AND ELDEVIK COLLECTION

In the midst of the Great Depression, as well-documented in hundreds of books and articles, Portlanders petitioned the federal Works Progress Administration to build a lodge at the line between green and white, tree and snow, at the 6,000-foot elevation of their beloved Mt. Hood. It took a year and a half to complete the 55,000 square-foot structure, a million dollars, 760,000 man hours and 400 men.

Timberline.

With much flair and fanfare, U.S. President Franklin D. Roosevelt dedicated Timberline Lodge on Sept. 28, 1937. The lodge opened for business Feb. 5, 1938. Lodge guests hiked to the treeless terrain above for long trips down, or skied in trees below the lodge, protected from weather. (A complete history of the lodge is documented in the book *Timberline Lodge: A Love Story*.)

Timberline was not the only ski lodge garnering headlines. The West's first ski resort, Sun Valley, invented the chairlift in 1936. The single-seater was designed by engineer Jim Curran, who had knowledge of building tramways that loaded bananas for shipping.

Timberline Lodge supporters saw the necessity of a chairlift and built their own. The Magic Mile cranked into operation Nov. 17, 1939, launching Timberline into an elite group of ski areas worldwide with a state-of-the-art lift. Timberline became the nation's first ski area with a chairlift built with steel towers.

George Henderson, Timberline's first public-relations man, named the single-seater chair.

"We called it the Magic Mile," explains Henderson. "There was the Miracle Mile,

John Elvrum (#52) and Hjalmer Hvam (#45) pose with other jumpers at a 1930s jump at Ski Bowl.

of course, Wilshire Boulevard in Los Angeles, the great strip to the beach at Santa Monica. We wanted to have a big promotion of the new chair. The name came up to call it Magic Mile after Miracle Mile. We gave out pins for people who could go the fastest down the Magic Mile runs. A mile a minute was the whole game."

The 18-minute ride on the $100,000 lift cost a skier $2. Powered by a steamship's diesel engine and boiler, the chair featured a lap blanket for each rider. The Silcox Hut upper terminus housed the bullwheel and a warming shelter.

Bamboo and leather ski-pole baskets prevented the bamboo poles from diving too deep in snow.

FRIENDS OF TIMBERLINE COLLECTION

Timberline Lodge

During the Great Depression, the U.S. government's Works Progress Administration (WPA) launched projects across the country in an effort to put the unemployed to work. Oregon's Timberline Lodge stands as the Northwest's grandest monument of the WPA and Oregon's artisans, craftsmen, engineers, architects, carpenters, sawyers, blacksmiths and many more.

As early as the 1920s, Portland developers hoped to build a tourist facility on Mt. Hood. Different groups petitioned the USFS with proposals that were turned down. In *Timberline Lodge: A Love Story*, Terence O'Donnell writes that Emerson Griffith and John Yeon chose a lodge site 2,200 feet above the village of Government Camp in 1934.

"The difficulty ... was to find backers," writes O'Donnell. "It was, after all, the Depression. Then ... the unexpected happened. Griffith, who had contacts in the Democratic party, was appointed Director of the Works Progress Administration in Oregon — and that meant money."

The USFS granted use of the land, Griffith applied for and received WPA money, and construction began June 13, 1936. Some 400 people built the lodge and were paid an average of 90 cents an hour.

"Some idea of the magnitude of the project may be obtained from the fact that it required 760,000 man-hours of labor to build Timberline Lodge," a WPA document states.

"Timberline Lodge is unusual ... because of its lavish use of indigenous materials ... and the wide scope ... given to the creative and inventive talents of native artists and craftsmen."

The 55,000 square-foot building was adorned with watercolor and oil paintings, murals, stained glass, wood carvings and marquetry, metalcraft, furniture and hand woven fabrics, created by Oregonians for the world.

On Sept. 28, 1937, U.S. President Franklin D. Roosevelt dedicated Timberline Lodge during a ceremony broadcast coast to coast by radio.

Timberline Lodge stands as the first WPA project where the government built and owned a hotel in a national forest.

Timberline Lodge, Mt. Hood National Forest, Timberline, Oregon   Altitude 6000 Feet. Altitude of Mountain 11,245 Feet

61

KOHNSTAMM COLLECTION

Hand painted postcard of the Lodge and original Mile.

Lodge envelope used late 1940s-60s

Skiers enjoyed the uphill conveyance, yet many simply took advantage of the trails down the mountain to Government Camp, affectionately called "Govy."

"In those days, we used to be able to leave skis propped up against the lodge, and they'd be there the next weekend when we came back!" recalls photographer Hugh Ackroyd.

Meanwhile on the north side, Hood River skiers climbed to Cloud Cap Chalet for the long ski down.

"A group of us would go up on Friday night and stay at Homestead Inn in 1936 to '38," recalls Betty Calmetts-Foster. My parents used to take us to Cooper Spur, and we'd ski up to Homestead. We had chaperones of course. The guys would stay on one end of the inn and gals on the other. We'd dance the *schottische*, a Scottish dance, to the Victrola. The next day we'd put climbers on and ski up to Cloud Cap. We'd ski down the fine trails, sometimes down to Parkdale and go to a movie then ski back up to Homestead."

They had the north slopes mostly to themselves although a group of promoters envisioned a tram from Cooper Spur to the mountain's summit. The project was never realized. What arose from the proposal was a broader awareness of wilderness preservation.

Concerned with self preservation, Norwegian skier Hjalmar Hvam envi-

sioned one of the most important devices ever invented for skiers. Hvam broke his leg while cornice jumping on Mt. Hood in 1937. As the oft-told story goes, Hvam lay in a Portland hospital bed recuperating.

"To live and not ski is a sad life," Hvam was quoted years later. "To ski and be afraid is still worth it. But to ski and have no fear — this is to be alive!" He came upon the idea of a releasable binding and within two years, patented it.

"In 1939 I said, 'There are too many broken legs from skiing,' so I invented the first safety release binding," said Hvam. "It will not come loose in racing or on ice. They never release when you ski but if you fall, your foot twists, and the Hvam golden cam toe binding releases."

1930s skiers in Government Camp pose in front of the Battle Axe Inn. Homestead claims at the turn of the century drew a few settlers to the area now known as Government Camp. The first hotel, the Mountain View House, was built in 1899 by O.C. Yocum.

Magic Mile

The first ski area in the U.S. to construct a chairlift using steel towers also forged a unique collaboration between the USFS, the WPA and Riblet Tramway Company to build the lift. The Magic Mile became "the only publicly owned and built lift in the country," recalls Ward Gano, retired USFS official.

It took two years to build the 4,953-foot lift that had a vertical rise of 996.5 feet. Turmoil arose, recalls Gano:

"One non-bidding tramway firm protested that a skier, positioning himself in front of a chair moving at 450-feet per minute, was risking a broken coccyx. In drafting a reply for the Chief, I had to turn to a medical book to find out what a coccyx was that was being threatened."

Just before the lift was to open in November, 1939, the first lift accident occurred.

"One of the workmen dismounted from a chair as to cause it to swing violently, snag on tower number two, force the rope out of the sheaves on that tower and cause it to lead out of the sheaves," recalls Gano. "No one was thrown from a chair and there were no injuries or serious damage. The incident triggered a rush of activity on preventive measures."

Ice build up on the chair and cable of the original Magic Mile forced the cable to drop within a few feet of skiers. "Twenty-four pounds of ice to the foot built up on the cable," recalls Hugh Ackroyd.

That year, Norway's Crown Prince Olav and Princess Martha traveled the West. The royal visitors, fine skiers themselves, dedicated the Magic Mile by screwing in gold-plated anchor bolts on a tower — a public-relations bonanza.

Opening day's ticket prices, recalls Gano, were 35 cents for a single ride; 50 cents round trip; $1 for three rides; and $2 for all day.

"I was not much of a skier when I went up to Timberline for a job," recalls Norm Weiner, who planned to work and save money for law school. "There was no manual for operating a chairlift. There were five people on the lift crew. The engineer had to get power to the lift from the power house, a separate power plant from the lodge's power plant — both built from dismantled WWI ships. I was at the lower terminal. It was my job to load people and collect money. There was a shack like an outhouse where I stood.

"When a person was ready to get on board the lift, he would ski up to the shack, give me money — quite often in silver which dropped in the snow — I'd give him a ticket and he'd move up to the boarding area. My job was to assist the person in getting on because people didn't have experience."

The Magic Mile operated until 1962 when it was replaced with the second Magic Mile, a double chair in a new location, west of the lodge.

A detachable high-speed quad, the Magic Mile Express, replaced the double seater in 1992.

Recreational skiing all but stopped when WWII and gas rationing closed ski hills nationwide. Timberline closed November 30, 1942. A few youngsters climbed to ski.

"Having seen the movie *Sun Valley Serenade*, I decided to start skiing," recalls then high school student John Carson.

"I bought some used ski equipment for $5, hitch-hiked to Mt. Hood and climbed to Timberline from Govy for the ski down," says Carson. This was 1944, and the road was closed because of the war. There was no gasoline for driving. My friend and I planned to stay over night at the old Timberline Cabin."

In Government Camp they met lodge caretaker, Ole Lein. He was skiing back to the lodge with supplies.

He suggested that the boys wait for him to break trail. By the time they arrived at Timberline, darkness engulfed the mountain.

"We could see ourselves floundering toward the cabin, maybe not finding it in the dark. So we backtracked and picked up the main trail to the lodge. We knocked on the door. 'You can't come in,' he said, so we spent the night, colder than the devil, in a blizzard. We slept in an enclave with a concrete floor. It was very uncomfortable."

The next day the sun emerged.

Jess Baird, Leavenworth Sports Club, leaving the take-off on Cascade Ski Club's B jump, January 24, 1937. Cascade also offered jumpers an A jump and a C jump.

Going to the Dogs

Several generations of St. Bernards graced Timberline Lodge's entry ways, foyer and slopes since the massive doors first opened. The first canine mascots, Lady and Bruel, patrolled the canyons and slopes gallantly. Sometimes they ventured further than their masters wished. Hank Lewis, a mountain climber and ski patroller recalls a 1937 incident:

"One day a guy by the name of Harold Chavis, a bellhop at the lodge wanted to climb the mountain. So we took off for the top. The dogs followed us up, the two St. Bernards, Lady and Bruel. We got to the top of Mt. Hood, and it came time to come back down. Well, like there often is, there was a stretch of ice in the chute. Lady put her snout down and skidded right on down the chute. Bruel was chicken. I figured that he'd come down after us, but he didn't."

The bellhop, Chavis had to hurry down to get to work, leaving Lewis to rescue the dog.

"I climbed back up the chute after the dog. I begged the dog, and cussed and damned him and couldn't move him. So I took a short rope from my pack and tied it around Bruel. That left just barely enough rope to tie to my belt. The dog weighed more than me, so I jumped backward, down the chute, tumbling with the dog. I repeated the performance until we finally hit the soft snow and stopped."

Thinking the dog would never climb the peak again, Lewis returned to his ski patrol duties. Two weeks later, the USFS placed fixed ropes in the chute. Lewis and the dogs went along for the climb.

"They did that back then for the climbers," he says of the anchored ropes. "Lady and Bruel followed us up again. And again Bruel would not come down. So I grabbed his collar and dragged him over the ice spots again."

A couple of weeks later, Lewis arrived at the lodge late on a Saturday afternoon. The lodge manager, Arthur Allen, said, "Hank, somebody left a dog on the summit."

I said, "The Mazamas are going up tomorrow. Let them get Bruel." The manager told me, "I want that dog down now!" I said "Okay, I'll go." I took off at 4:30 to climb the mountain. I made it in two-and-a-half hours from Timberline to the summit, far from a record, but not a bad time. I got up there, grabbed Bruel and dragged him down the chute again."

Exhausted, Lewis figured the incidents would be forgotten. "There was a stringer from the *Oregonian*. She wanted a photo and a story. I said no way. But she wrote a story and put it in the paper anyway, and it hit the Associated Press [wire service]. I received fan mail and a lot of ribbing. I brought that damn dog off the summit three times!"

Timberline's first canine mascots, Lady and Bruel.

PHOTOS: FRIENDS OF TIMBERLINE COLLECTION

"We skied down in the deep new snow, more of an exercise in walking than skiing."

The post-war 1940s saw 21 new T-bars and lifts constructed in America, including Jack Baldwin's rope tow near the Cooper Spur Junction, built in 1946. As with many of the country's established ski areas, Timberline reopened late 1945.

Helped by six feet of snow in Rhododendron in the winter of 1949, skiers again dashed to Mt. Hood. They found a ski world transforming into a business world helped by a positive economy, enthusiastic veterans of the Tenth Mountain Division, and thriving experimentation in ski technique, instruction and equipment.

By 1950, skiing had settled into the American psyche and defined winter for thousands. Howard Head made his first production skis, selling them for $85 a pair. People called them "cheater" skis. Henke introduced the first buckle boot. Double chairlifts became the norm.

As skiers snowplowed and stem christied at four alpine sites on Mt. Hood, new areas developed nationwide competing for skiers' dollars. Timberline's near demise arose not from competitors but from within. According to USFS documents, a scurrilous lodge manager, Charles Slaney, allowed the facility to fall into ruin.

Donald Sterling, Jr., a young journalist for the *Oregon Journal*, recalls February 17, 1955:

"The weather was gloomy at Timberline the day of the closure. My most memorable experience at Timberline came on what literally was the lodge's darkest day since World War II. It was overcast and gray, but not snowing.

"When I arrived around noon, the inside of the building was totally dark. The electric co-op that supplied Timberline with electricity had cut off the power for non-payment of its bill. It was possible to find one's way around inside only because in the chilly entrance lobby a few candles flickered in various drinking glasses and other containers set around the cold fireplace. The guests, if any there had been, had left.

"The only person I remember finding in the building was Slaney, dressed in a war-surplus ski parka, scurrying around gathering up bedding, dishes and other furnishings in cartons to carry away with him. That was the darkness that brought along the dawn."

The lodge remained closed until July 1, 1955, when Richard L. Kohnstamm, armed with buckets, brooms and financial savvy, flipped on the lights. ⨈

Painter Eliza Barchus' image of Mt. Hood was printed on a 1905 postcard. "Mt. Hood was a distant, inaccessible, beautiful thing, viewed from afar until Timberline Lodge was built," says Portland native Peggy Arthur Rector.

FRIENDS OF TIMBERLINE COLLECTION

The chapter's end character, the "end bug," is an Anasazi symbol for a flying goose. This symbol adorns Timberline's headhouse, atop the chimney as the iron weather vane.

Sheaves and Ropes

Opposite page: Under a full moon, a lone skier makes tracks to Timberline Lodge, circa 1938.

Lift Tickets: "People used to save their old lift tickets attached to their ski jackets until they had a couple dozen tickets hanging from their zipper," recalls long-time Timberline employee Steve Stubbs. "You traded them in for special Timberline pins — 50 tickets for a big pin."

Skiing's beginnings as a raucous and rambling sport attracted adventurers as untamed as the slopes they schussed. As skiers cultivated their technique, ski lifts and equipment became more refined. That evolution began with airborne jumpers and comes full circle with airborne snowboarders.

In the 1920s and 30s, skiers were washboard tough.

"The ski jumpers were mostly Norwegians and often of the hard-drinking crowd," says Norwegian jumper John Elvrum. "They were often rowdy and behaved like a bunch of ruffians."

If the jumpers' etiquette rivaled barge captains' manners, early ski slopes and lifts had the demeanor of a typhoon. Ski entrepreneurs sought to tame winter's forces, *and* the skiers. The taming came twofold: mechanized lifts and mechanized grooming.

While some skiers and boarders still hike to schuss, most savor the 60 years

ACKROYD PHOTO

The Salmon River Rope Tow, April 1948.

of lift rides. However, not all ski-area contrivances endure. Despite the Magic Mile, the Otto Lang tow, Salmon River tow and a platter pull in Pucci's Glade, until 1948 skiers had to park in Government Camp and hike or shuttle to Timberline's lifts.

"Timberline, the $1 million structure, a gift from Uncle Sam, stands almost in isolation, so acute is the winter road problem," stated a 1948 editorial in the *Oregon Journal*.

Portland investors proposed a Skiway to Timberline using logging technology.

"The proposed 'aerial streetcar'… will supply … a service the U.S. government hasn't been able to perfect in 10 years of costly endeavor," wrote the 1948 editorialist.

The Skiway began operation in January 1951, nearly two years after a new and much improved road opened to Timberline.

"In an ill-fated attempt to bypass the road and connect the town to the lodge, an extraordinary aerial tram was created, composed of two city buses winding their way up the cables in a high-wire act worthy of the Big Top," Mary and Joe Gmuender write in *Ski Area Management*.

"You sat next to the engine and next to the cable and a big drum that the cable wound on," recalls local skier Charlie Sperr. "When the bus came down after leaving a tower, it would speed up then kick in gear and really get noisy. It took probably 20 minutes to a half hour to get to Timberline. Hell, you could drive up there faster."

The new road to Timberline opened the summer of 1949, and with it, bus rides for 50 cents — half the price of the Skiway.

John West, a Government Camp native, recalls that while picking huckleberries under the Skiway, he bet his brother that the bus wouldn't make it over the next tower.

"And sometimes it didn't!" says West. "They'd have to back it down and try again."

GOOD FOR ONE-WAY PASSAGE ON
Skiway COACH
GOV'T. CAMP, ORE.
Sold Subject to Tariff Regulations
on File with U.S. Forest Service.
GLOBE TICKET CO., OF WASH., TACOMA
016593

FRIENDS OF TIMBERLINE COLLECTION

America's second aerial passenger tram carried skiers and sightseers between Government Camp and Timberline, 1951-56.

FRIENDS OF TIMBERLINE COLLECTION

As the Skiway failed in the mid-1950s, so did Timberline. Manager Charles Slaney had neglected to pay the power bill, and damaged the chairlift so that Lloyd's of London canceled their insurance.

In stepped Richard L. Kohnstamm.

The 29-year-old social worker from New York secured management of the failing lodge and its faltering ski operation on the southern slopes of Mt. Hood.

On April 28, 1955, USFS Regional Forester J. Herbert Stone awarded a 10-year operating permit to Kohnstamm. The Columbia University graduate was the eighth manager for the 18-year-old hotel. Previous managers (Larry McLean, Arthur Allen, Fred VanDyke, William Temple, George North, John McFadden and Slaney) found operation of the 55,000-square-foot behemoth cumbersome and financially unviable.

On Kohnstamm's first day at work, "I found filth, unworkable ski lifts and broken furniture and fixtures."

He immediately began simultaneous campaigns to clean and refurbish the lodge, and rebuild and revive the ski lifts and tows to reclaim Timberline's honor as a showplace of Oregon.

Kohnstamm frequented Timberline before leasing the hotel and ski venture from the USFS. "Some employees wanted me to take over the lodge a year earlier," he recalls. "One fellow, Jim Duncan, told me it'd take $10,000 to reopen the lodge. It cost $10,000 to open the

"This is the condition of the lift that I found on my first day of work," says R.L. Kohnstamm. **"The broken bullwheel from the Magic Mile lay in pieces on the floor of Silcox Hut. We never knew how it was broken."**

Early 1960s ski wax from Joie Smith's Alpine Ski Shop in Rhododendron.

Skiers behind Multorpor's Tucker Sno-Cat get a ride from the parking lot to T-bar Hill.

Mile and another $3,000 just to clean up the inside of the lodge."

Skiers wore Molitor or Kastinger boots and listened to Chuck Berry's hit "Mabellene." Savvy skiers used Austrian-made ski poles. Sohms Red slicked wooden skis. This post World War II era saw the number of ski areas in North America grow vigorously. Fifty-five chairlifts existed in the U.S. by 1955.

A flurry of innovations from metal skis to buckle boots affected the post-war ski experience. Oregon's Hjalmer Hvam improved upon his patented safety binding. His advertisements shouted, "Hvooming with Hvam."

While the growing ski industry tried the stem christy and the wedelin counter rotation technique, Mt. Hood ski areas struggled with deep snows.

"When we installed the Pucci lift in 1955, it wasn't designed for the amount of snow here," says Kohnstamm. "The lower terminal was too low, and we had to dig it out often."

Ski areas across the country installed double chairlifts, adding a new twist to skiing — the novelty and romance of sitting shoulder-to-shoulder with another skier.

"Rope tows are still the most economic way to get bodies up hill but a very tricky method," says Kohnstamm. "There were lots of near strangulations by scarf or hair."

Interestingly enough, it was Kohnstamm's second cousin, Ernest Constam, who invented the first lift exclusively for ski sport. The Zurich engineer designed and built the J-bar in 1934 and Lieni Fopp, whose nephew, Martin Fopp, taught skiing at Timberline, financed it. Constam later doubled capacity by inventing the T-bar in 1936.

By the lodge's 25th anniversary, the queen dowager Magic Mile chairlift was retired for a double-seater installed in a new site, west of Timberline Lodge. Skiing down the Mile, one could not help but notice the activity below on Tom, Dick & Harry Mountain, called Ski Bowl.

"We were recreational skiing and having a good day," recalls Bud Fields. "The lift was fast and dangerous. We used a metal hook to ride the tow." Skiers Dick Irvin, Bud Fields, Rees Stevenson and LaVern "Hap" Hughes, take a break at the Ski Bowl warming hut in 1947.

Carl Reynolds bought Multorpor in 1950 and Ski Bowl in 1964.

"All there was was a tiny warming hut where the East Lodge is now," says Reynold's son Chuck. "And there was a rope tow. His first project was to build the T-bar on Multorpor Mountain where now there is a double chair, closest to the lodge. The original tow was fast and dangerous, the Jump Hill rope, largely supplanted when the Constam T-bar went up.

"The Bunny Basin rope tow remained in place for a number of years, close to the parking lot and Cascade jump hill. You'd put skis on in the parking lot and ski up to the lodge."

Reynolds merged Multorpor and Ski Bowl into both a beginner's mecca and the hard-core skiers' hang out. Until a Riblet double chair was installed in 1955, accomplished skiers shouldered their army-surplus skis and hiked to the bottom of the Upper Bowl and the rope tow.

"Those were the days of ski tows," says Bud Fields. "Ski Bowl had a rope tow. You wore a belt around your waist with a metal hook and attached the hook to the rope tow. Boyd French invented that hook. We had good days skiing Ski Bowl."

He recalls paying $2.50 a day to ride a tow powered by a truck engine.

Multorpor's T-bar, built about 1950 on T-bar Hill. "If you were skiing back to the Warming Hut from the Bunny Basin slopes where the ski school, rope tows, and the out houses were, you skied through the skiers riding the T-bar," recalls Chuck Reynolds. "You had to gauge your run to go between the skiers who were riding up. If you had a packed run and poled hard, you had just enough speed to make it up the grade to the warming hut." The T-bar has since been replaced with a double chair.

"We tried everything up there for summer skiing," recalls John West who built a portable lift using grammar-school seats. Some of the seats now adorn Charlie's Mountain View bar in Government Camp.

"When they ran out of gas for the rope tow, we had to pack in gas. We used G.I. gas cans, put them on our backs in a knapsack and hiked in from the highway. It took a half hour to hike in without the gas can and an extra 15 minutes with it."

They still bought a lift ticket, he recalls.

"Ski Bowl only ran weekends," says Fields. "Boyd French was a casual operator. When the snow melted, the towers for the tow just fell over. The towers were not buried in dirt, just planted in the snow. So that was the end of the season."

As if Kohnstamm couldn't get enough of winter, he longed for an endless ski season. He looked to Europe and the high Alps for summer skiing

successes. He opened the first Summer Racing Camp in 1956.

"Americans weren't interested in summer skiing," says Kohnstamm. "The French had summer skiing, and they unabashedly said that they were the better racers because of it."

From the top of the Mile, racers rode in the Tucker Sno-Cats then upon a variety of portable lift contraptions to 10,000 feet: Camp 10. Portable lifts resembled rummage-sale bargains. There was the cable attached to grammar-school seats on skis. There were pomas and rope tows, all removed at summer's end.

Finally, in 1979, at the urging of U.S. Ski Team Coach Hank Tauber, Kohnstamm built Palmer Chairlift. It opened

Autographs and Sunglasses

While filming a made-for-television movie about skyjacker D.B. Cooper, actor George Kennedy lived in Timberline Lodge. One exhaustive and frustrating day, he stomped into the Cascade Dining Room fuming, "Making movies isn't all autographs and sunglasses!"

Neither is the making of a ski resort.

A certain glamour exists in running a ski operation. The locals ski every day, get first tracks in powder, and have next year's ski equipment. It's a well-polished myth.

Failures and *faux pas* might deter a lesser sport. Skiing endured and flourished despite flops. R.L. Kohnstamm and his son, Jeff, consider the blunders-and-breaks part of doing business at 6,000 feet.

A folly from the beginning was a platter pull built in Pucci's Glade.

"A platter pull built in Pucci's Glade below Timberline Lodge (had) a reported cost of $36,000," states a photo caption in the January 23, 1955, issue of the *Oregonian*. "The device never operated."

When Kohnstamm took over the lodge and ski area in 1955, the Magic Mile's bullwheel lay in pieces on the floor of Silcox Hut. He replaced the bullwheel in time for ski season.

Storms raged on the equipment. Ice build-ups made sails out of chairlifts, eventually ripping some chairs from the cable. Work crews found pieces of the lift in White River Canyon.

"Things stay pretty together with winds up to 80 miles per hour if we can keep the lift moving," says Mountain Manager, Bill Brett. "But as soon as the power goes out and the lift stops, the ice builds up and you have a big sail. Every few years a big storm will blow the rope off of one or two dozen towers."

As winds calm and all seems safe, an avalanche of snow slides off the lodge roof crashes through the windows on the east side of the foyer. The mop-up is anything but glamourous.

When stars ski at Timberline, as they often do, the royal treatment sometimes includes a Sno-Cat ride up the mountain.

"In 1975, we were filming some skiing," recalls Olympian Billy Kidd. "Kohnstamm drives me up in a cat and parks it across the hill. When he starts the engine again, the vibration makes the cat slide sideways, downhill. 'RRR, rrr,' I hear. Something's wrong. The engine won't start. We're picking up speed. I said, 'Sorry, Dick. I don't want to stick around.' I'm on the uphill side and jump. He jumps, too. We watch the cat slide faster and faster. It rolls like a tow truck and ends up wrecked in a crevasse."

During the first Trans Antarctic Expedition, the crew trained on Mt. Hood. They rescued their Tucker Sno-Cat from this Antarctic crevasse.

"It was one of our jobs to get the old Spryte out," recalls Steve Haugk. "We were down in a crevasse hanging from ropes to take it apart, piece by piece. We hired a helicopter and flew the pieces down to the lodge and rebuilt it."

Mechanics worked long nights. They repaired chairs that were squashed flat because somebody had forgotten to open the doors of Silcox Hut upper terminal. They dug presidential candidate Adlai Stevenson out of a foggy canyon when Timberline's P.R. manager drove the Democrat off a bank in a Sno-Cat.

After all the splicing, welding, pounding and greasing, they never consider that ski area work is all autographs and sunglasses.

exclusively for summer skiing.

Meanwhile, on the other side of Mt. Hood, Hood River skiers looked for higher slopes with more consistent snows than their well-loved Cooper Spur where a lift ticket in 1967 went for $5. Jack Baldwin, George Howell and others surveyed beyond Cooper Spur.

"Skiing was an allied secondary sport to climbing for winter sports people here," says Bill Pattison of Hood River. "The residents of Hood River did a lot of playing in the Homestead area. They had races and built a jump that eventually became Cooper Spur. A group from Hood River wanted to put together a new area. The forest service people were very attentive."

"Jack (Baldwin) started looking for a ski area about 1960," recalls Virginia

"We contributed 40 years to skiing at Cooper Spur," says Virginia Baldwin. "Now there is the annual Jack Baldwin Memorial Ski Race with 180 participants."

Baldwin. "He and Dick Ewald and George Howell were up on the mountain several times a summer for four years before they found the meadows area."

Surveys, feasibility studies and research satisfied the USFS that a new ski area could work.

Lift construction began in 1967, not with the Hood River group but by Portland investors headed by Franklin Drake who had won the 30-year USFS contract to develop the new area.

As is her penchant, the mountain did little to cooperate when Mt. Hood Meadows Oregon, Ltd. built lifts, day lodge and road.

"An extremely dry summer caused forest fires in the Rocky Mountains and Eastern Oregon, which drew helicopters away to fight the fires," recalls Drake. "The same unusually dry weather caused the contractor building Highway 35 to year-round standards to shut down for part of the summer. He missed the deadline for opening Highway 35 for the 1967-68 winter from the Government Camp side."

By the time six million skiers visited the 800 ski areas across North America

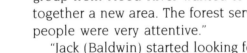

A helicopter flies towers during construction of the Blossom chairlift. "We flew 19 or 20 towers in one hour and 20 minutes," recalls Steve Haugk. "We saw a storm coming in and had to work faster than the storm front."

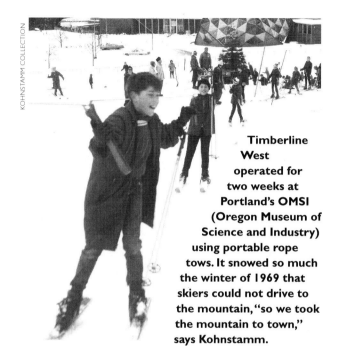

Timberline West operated for two weeks at Portland's OMSI (Oregon Museum of Science and Industry) using portable rope tows. It snowed so much the winter of 1969 that skiers could not drive to the mountain, "so we took the mountain to town," says Kohnstamm.

in the 1970s, annual spending on the sport "broke the billion dollar barrier," according to the *Encyclopedia of Skiing*.

By 1979, annual skier visits were over a million for Oregon and continued to rise for two decades, joining a national trend. After 1.5 million skier visits statewide in 1994-95, the growth trend leveled.

Ski area managers nationwide feared that skiing's heyday had passed. Few anticipated the impact of skiing's wild child, snowboarding.

The Pacific Northwest leads the country in percentage of total boarder visits according to the Kottke study provided by the Pacific Northwest Ski Areas Association.

"Snowboarding represents a significant segment of the ski industry not only in skier visits generated, but in lesson participation and equipment rentals," the report finds.

No matter what people use to slide down the mountain, weather continues to force creative solutions on outdoor equipment.

"The new Palmer Express detachable-quad chair is extremely innovative," says Jon Tullis, Timberline's Director of Public Affairs. "The top terminal is actually inside the mountain. It has a bypassable midway station. Also unique is the 90-degree loading and unloading which has proven to be very user-friendly."

Easing the uphill route was only half of the evolution of ski mechanisms. Skiers and ski area operators learned early that they needed smoother and safer slopes. Slope grooming began back in the 1920s. The ski jumpers found that they needed to pack out their takeoffs and out-runs for successful jumps and landings. The jumpers invented slope grooming.

"Volunteers were asked to help pack the snow on the big hill, making a solid

Prior to WWII, the MHSP convinced the USFS to install hand-crank trail phones for emergencies. They were replaced in 1975 with underground cable and two emergency phones. "The old crank-up trail phones were mounted so they could be moved up and down depending on snow depth," recalls Joie Smith.

Skiing the Glade

While the Glade Trail slides gently downward from Timberline, ungroomed and unpatrolled, at one time skiers clogged the route on Saturdays, heading down to Government Camp and Hill's Place.

The old one-way road up to Timberline, the East Leg Road remained closed to private vehicles, as did the West Leg Road down the hill.

"When Timberline started up, I drove bus the first four winters," says Bill Lenz. "Drove an old Packard bus. Mt. Hood Stages and Grayline had 15 buses running up there, three rides for a dollar. We had one guy from Portland who used to jump on the back of the bus, onto the ski rack so he didn't have to pay. People all knew he was back there, so they'd get me to stop the bus. I'd always stop about half way up the road so he'd have a long walk."

The route down defied many beginners.

"I learned to ski on the Glade Trail in the early 60s," recalls Scott Farleigh. "Parents drove us up to Timberline in the morning and picked us up at Government Camp at the end of the day. We hitch hiked up the

Schnee Volglie ski club pin.

mountain from the Huckleberry Inn after racing down the trail. On a good day we could get in eight or nine runs."

Like many before him, Farleigh borrowed wooden skis "with ancient cable bindings." No need to learn to turn, he says. They followed the ruts.

"I brought a girlfriend along one day and promised to teach her my technique," he says. "She made it down one time, but after the nasty trip in the ruts, she refused to ever see me again!"

If romance wasn't in store for the Glade, humor was.

"The Kandabeer Race got started in a session in the Blue Ox Bar," recalls Jack Vidoni, member of Schnee Vogli ski club. "Three or four guys decided they would chug in the Blue Ox, and the first guy to Govy won. They skied to Battle Ax Inn, drank a beer, and there was the first winner."

The original plaque dates 1950. Lucky McKenney won nine years in a row.

"At one time it started in the Ramshead Bar," says Jack Vidoni. "Lucky used to rent a room in the lodge and drink a beer then go into his room and put on his skis and ski out the window. There was snow up on the roof. It'd give him a hell of a start."

Teams dressed as a six-pack, or an army tank. One cold character streaked the race painted up red, white and blue like a K2 ski.

"It was custom to drink a beer, put on skis, ski half way down, drink another beer then a third beer at the bottom, in under ten minutes over 3.5 miles," says Charlie Sperr.

For liability reasons, the race ceased about 1990 but not before racers hoodwinked each other.

"People would hide skis of fellow racers or put peanut butter on ski bases," laughs Vidoni. "I pushed Kenny Van Dyke into a tree well during the race one year."

The trail itself is a USFS creation connecting the old Blossom wagon road with a series of natural glades. Glade Trail skiing improved significantly when Lou Russell bought his own $8,000 Tucker Sno-Cat in 1960.

"We were waiting in a lift line one day, and I asked my dad if we could rent Timberline's Sno-Cat for a ride up," recalls Russell's son Scott. "He came home with a Sno-Cat a month later! It was his hobby to groom the Glade which significantly reduced the number of accidents on the trail."

For 20 years, the Russells smoothed bumps and washboards on the Glade.

Among the various contraptions people slid on down the trail, none is as unusual as Skosh People's trail loafer.

"I've skied the Glade on flat-bottom leather shoes," he says. "I'd turn around backwards and do the whole trail on my shoes on sheer ice!"

foundation for the new snows to come," wrote Corey Gustafsson in 1931 for the Cascade Ski Club yearbook. "The call for help was answered by men, women and children, who either on skis or foot tramped the snow, four feet deep, until it was packed fairly hard."

While boot packing worked, it was a slow, sweaty task. During construction of Timberline Lodge, an engineer working on the lodge created the first snow vehicle invented for ski-area use.

"A man named Davidson got the bright idea there could be an over-snow machine," says George Henderson. "He had the idea of a great wide track with a little cab and sled pulled behind it. He called it the 'Snowcat.' His principle was to have one wide track and the engine inside so that it couldn't high center. He began using it the winter of 1936-37."

While Davidson's creation of a snow machine visualized travel and hauling, it inadvertently became one of the first grooming machines in the West. Ski racer and filmmaker Dick Durrance recalls the 1939 U.S. Nationals down-mountain course above Timberline Lodge.

"We always hiked the race courses, side stepping to pack out our run," says Durrance who won the race. "A lot of the racers got in the one-and-a-half foot deep track made by the snow cat."

Woodcut circa 1938 from a WPA booklet about Timberline Lodge.

A White Straight Jacket

"The development, construction and operation of a major ski area provides many challenges," says Franklin Drake who developed Mt. Hood Meadows from the ground up. "To conquer those challenges through the weather extremes found in the mountains requires a lot of teamwork, tenacity and a strong character.

"If you don't start with strong character, these experiences will build strong character. Along with the strong character goes a good sense of humor.

"Two key players in the early construction of Meadows were Barney Metzger, general superintendent, and Big John West, chairlift builder and mountain manager. In the 1968 winter, our second season of operation, we had up to 32 feet of snow under and around portions of our number one chair.

"Metzger was observing Big John from a distance, adjusting sheaves on top of one tower. Just at that instant, Big John slipped and fell head first into the deep, soft snow. He was buried, almost out of sight, upside down in a cold, white straight jacket. It took Barney some time to get to Big John and remove much of the snow by hand.

"Big John's first words: 'This is a drill, and you took too long.'"

Although racers utilized the narrow route, most skiers endured natural, ragged, untamed slopes.

Another western inventor, Emmitt Tucker had his own idea of winter transport, building a trackless model in 1931.

"Emmitt's first machine was used for over-snow transport," says Bruce Sampson of Tucker Sno-Cats in Medford, Oregon. "There was no track. It had a big auger that acted as a screw, pulling its way over the snow. It had an Indian motorcycle engine, carried six people and pulled 36 others behind it."

Tucker's initial machines satisfied logging operators and soon became indispensible to the ski industry. Since 1942 some 6,500 Tucker Sno-Cats roamed the ski slopes and cross-country trails of the continent, figuring in on search and rescues, logging sites and utility projects.

On Mt. Hood's north slopes, others experimented with snow machines. Ted and Wesley Weygandt purchased army surplus vehicles.

"We had four M-26 Army Weasels, a cheap version of a track layer," says Ted Weygandt. "We transported people from the end of the road up to Cooper Spur, about one and three quarter miles. We also took passengers like the Portland Snow Shoe Club up to Cloud Cap Inn."

They charged 50 cents per person.

FRIENDS OF TIMBERLINE COLLECTION, MACONE PHOTO

Tucker Sno-Cat in action.

Two machines pulling Bombardier trailers hauled two dozen people.

"Wesley and I gave up our venture with the snow cats after three-and-a-half years of not making anything more than expenses," adds Weygandt.

Until the early 1960s however, the snow machines were used primarily for uphill transportation. Timberline's Ski School Director Lorne O'Connor suggested trying slope maintenance, something he'd seen in Eastern Canada.

"No grooming and heck, Timberline didn't even have a ski map," says O'Con-

The first over-the-snow vehicle created for ski area use was built by an engineer working on the building of Timberline in 1936. It was nicknamed "Snow Kitty."

nor. "We had cats but used them to go uphill. We groomed wall to wall on Pucci so people would have fun skiing."

Drum rollers, dragged chains, slat rollers, gang rollers and chain-link fences bumped and jibed over the snow. Sometimes they left ice chunks or washboards behind.

"We had an old wooden slat roller, then after that, a culvert," says retired Timberline Mountain Manager Steve Haugk. "We made several things, even a gang roller, three rollers, one wide and two smaller ones to pull behind a cat."

Mogul exterminators they became. Ski areas across the continent destroyed bumps only to have them sprout like ragweed in a pasture. Finally Tucker's

MACONE PHOTO

WEYGANDT PHOTO

competitor, Thiokol developed a solution in the late 1970s.

"Tucker had been the mainstay of the industry," says Haugk. "In 1963 or '64, we had the first Thiokol rubber track machine. We had probably one of the first rotary tillers in the Northwest, one of the Pack Masters with compactor bars like a beavertail where you drag through and push down on the snow rather than use a roller to smooth over the snow."

"Smooth" has several definitions for a snow groomer.

"We had been letting the bumps build up on Phlox for a week or so for a mogul

"Emmitt Tucker was demonstrating one of his Sno-Cats," recalls Kohnstamm. "He tried to climb up the bank with the cat. He was showing off a bit and the cat slipped sideways and crashed in the parking lot."

contest," recalls Artie Speicher. "All of the groomers knew about it, so they were not grooming it. A certain groomer was out by himself, and thought that he would do an excellent job on Phlox. And he did. He was so proud of what a good job that he had done that he was beaming in the morning for us to go look at it."

"This was during one of those bump contests with $10,000 in prize money," says former groomer Larry Berger. "I forgot all about the bump contest and cut 'em all down. I told Artie that I'd made Phlox as slick as a baby's behind. Then I remembered the bump contest, but it was 4 a.m. so I went home. Bill Brett, my boss, called me and told me to come back to work and bring a shovel."

It takes much more than a shovel for snow farmers on Mt. Hood to manage Mother Nature's abundance. While some resorts artificially inseminate winter with snowmaking, Timberline learned to finagle winter's mistrals. After years of pushing snow out of the parking lot, Timberline's crews discovered how to shape the hillocks surrounding the parking lot and allow wind to sweep the pavement clean.

At the millennium, Timberline's mechanics join Bombardier's engineers to create a machine capable of plowing out lift lines under the Magic Mile and Palmer when deep snow buries hanging chairs. Like ski manufacturers that test next year's models on Timberline's summer slopes, snow groomer manufacturers test new models on Palmer snowfield.

A fleet of $150,000 machines now break up ice, remove air from snow and make it more dense so skiers float on top. And after all the grooming and snow farming to smooth the natural terrain, snowboarders yearn for the irregularities of yesteryear. Some even hike uphill like their wild and woolly predecessors, the ski jumpers.

ACKROYD PHOTO

Timberline employees try to dig out from deep snows at Silcox Hut. The top terminal of the Magic Mile was named after USFS Chief Forester, F.A. Silcox.

On Snow and Snowing

Memories may fade as snow melts yet many skiers profess that snow used to be deeper and the snow line lower "in the old days."

One indication of weather change is the Snowline Motel in Rhododendron, named for the elevation at which snow remains on the ground much of the winter.

"In 1949 we had six feet of snow in Rhody," says Joie Smith, life-long Rhododendron resident. "The motel was named for the permanent snow line. And it's the start of the big climb up the mountain."

Nancy Spencer recalls that people chained up in Rhododendron to drive on

FRIENDS OF TIMBERLINE COLLECTION

Otto Lang skiing in 1937.

snow. "We didn't have good snow-removal equipment back then," she adds.

In 1956, snow fell a remarkable 28 days, non-stop.

"It snowed like crazy my first winter," recalls Kohnstamm. "Then in 1960, it didn't snow until Christmas vacation. It nearly broke us without snow."

One winter was so cold that he had trouble keeping the massive building heated.

"We turned off heat to the swimming pool to help heat the lodge," he recalls. "The pool froze. We threw logs into the pool to help prevent cracking the pool's foundation."

"Certainly the weather is our biggest challenge," says Bill Brett Timberline Mountain Manager. "Incidents like deropements from the wind or a couple feet of rime ice on the lifts pose a big challenge. The next challenge is operating 50 weeks a year, and we're still trying to figure out the best way to get all the work done."

One of the few storms that closed Timberline Road and buried the lodge, also kept Lodge Support employee Steve Buchan from a date.

"I'd worked four nights, and headed down the Glade Trail," recalls Buchan of

the winter of 1980. "I'd only been on the trail one time, and it had taken me ten minutes to ski down on my alpine skis.

"I traverse out to the Mile. As I push along, snow builds up in front of me. I think I'm still pretty close to the lodge, so I turn around and try to go back up hill. I can't go up hill. So I turn back, figure I have all day.

"It's still dumping as I go. It gets to the point where I can't keep going. The snow builds up to my chest. I take poles and pull skis up and go over the pile and do the pole thing for hours. I'm fully sweaty and tired. I don't think I told anyone where I was going. It seemed so casual to me.

"After four hours, I tell myself I'm pretty macho. I'm a man. I can do this. I have no idea how far Govy is. There are points where I don't cry but think I'm gonna die. I come to an emergency pole and phone and went over to call for help. The phone is fully dead, hadn't worked for years apparently.

"Five hours into the trip, I tell myself, enough with the man stuff. It's time to live. Another hour and finally I see a house. I'm fully tattered. I get to Huckleberry Inn and catch the last bus up to Timberline and go right to work. That night the road closed. It was the last trip the bus made for five days."

Boots and skis tromped snow on the jump hills of the 1920s, 30s and 40s, drum and slat rollers compressed runs in the 50s and 60s and machine packers and hydrostatic tillers buffed them in the 70s, 80s and 90s. Now mechanical creations carve up the corduroy and dredge trenches.

Scorpions, Pipe Dragons, Pipe Shredders and Half Pipe Groomers, fairy-tale creations for a snowboarding generation scoop, chop and sculpt the terrain for nearly half of the ticket purchasers. "In 1990 we built summer's first half pipe," says John Ingersoll of High Cascade Snowboard Camp. "Most snowboarders might take a run on the lifts then go over to our half pipe.

"That summer, Dick Kohnstamm came up in a cat and stood there just looking at the half pipe. 'You know this reminds me of when there were no ski lifts running,' he began. 'People willing to hike for turns. I haven't seen this since the 1950s when slalom skiers would hike up after the lifts closed.' The boarders have chair access but they choose to hike. Kohnstamm's employees were all saying, 'This is going to be

a pain. The boarders will want more cat time to make half pipes.' But Kohnstamm knew that snowboarding was going to be the next wave."

With million-dollar machines glistening in the snowfields and skiers and boarders edging and gliding their way downhill, snowsports continue to evolve. Backcountry ski mountaineers seek skiing's roots in uncultured slopes. They climb with state-of-the-art skis and climbing skins to pristine snowfields. As they master the antique telemark turn, they complete the full circle of a century of skiing on Mt. Hood. ⛏

Groomer Jeff Flood driving Chris Perkins (from Bombardier) in the Bombardier HPG, a "Half Pipe Groomer."

Daily bus service booklet from 1939.

Yumping, Yodeling & Nose Grabs

FOUND IN TIMBERLINE'S ATTIC

Opposite Page: In flight off Multorpor's ski jump in the 1930s.

Ski jumpers with heavy Norwegian accents and heavier eight-foot hickories, defied gravity and other laws, occasionally. Ski jumping and the "yumpers," deserve credit for ski competition's popularity in the Pacific Northwest. The Northwest warrants credit for fostering a climate of innovation and inspiration to cultivate competition.

The first Winter Olympic Games at Chamonix, France, in 1924, publicized ski sport like no earlier event. Jumping and cross-country races pitted country against country. Norway swept the medals.

Norwegians sought jobs in the mines, the forests and the railroads of the North American West. They brought their jumping talents and their 25-pound skis to the new country.

Highway paving on U.S. 26 in 1922, and snowplowing in 1926 allowed winter access to Government Camp and

allowed winter enthusiasts to build jump hills. They sponsored national races and local racing debuts.

"John Elvrum came from Norway," says his nephew Jarle Eldevik. "When he arrived in Portland, about 1930 he found it quite natural to join in with the jumpers who entered tournaments in the region. The Cascade Ski Club quickly embraced him as their own and promoted him as the 'Great New Find' of the year. They pitted him against all comers."

Drawing spectators to jumps at Mt. Hood's Swim, Multorpor Hill and Hood River's Ski Club Tournaments, the new sport launched into headlines and hearts. People walked two miles through snow to witness the high-flying skiers.

ELVRUM AND ELDEVIK COLLECTION

"Here, on January 12, 1930, in biting cold weather, was held the first championship tournament," wrote Harold Lee, then President of Cascade Ski Club. Of the Swim jump hill he continued, "Despite the inaccessibility of this hill, almost two miles from the highway, and the unfavorable weather, ... some 2,500 spectators attended meets."

When Cascade Ski Club opened Multorpor Hill, competitors recorded jumps of 196 feet off "a scientifically correct jumping hill" with a 38 percent grade, according to Cascade's Corey Gustafsson.

Mt. Hood's jump hills were by no means the longest, but drew the best jumpers from the West.

"Portland would pour out many people to watch a jump meet," says Cana-

ELVRUM AND ELDEVIK COLLECTION

dian jumping champion Earl Pletsch. "I'd look down the in-run to the take-off, and as I jumped, I could see all the people looking up at me with their mouths open. It was a thrill."

Brash, bold and fearless, the jumpers enchanted spectators. They also established *après* ski.

"Someone had promised liquor to the yumpers after a Seattle event," recalls 90-year-old John Elvrum. "This was during Prohibition. The yumpers had to wait until after the judges finished with the results. As it turned out, the judges had begun tasting the bonus, and while deliberating the final scores, finished off the allotted beverage. The yumpers were left nothing. They protested loudly and many swore never to come back to yump in a Seattle Ski Club tournament. I told the judges myself that I was so insulted, they would never see me yump in the Seattle area again."

Cascade jumpers Elvrum, Hjalmar Hvam and Corey Gustafsson held national rankings. Elvrum won all his tournaments in 1931 and set the nation's amateur record at 240 feet in 1934 at Big Pines, California. They hitchhiked or borrowed automobiles to get to the jump hills of Leavenworth, Washington or Revelstoke, British Columbia. Ski clubs hosted their stay in exchange for preparing the jumps.

Ski clubs including Cascade Ski Club, Bend Skyliners, Seattle Ski Club, Leavenworth Ski Club, Cle Elum Ski Club, Hood River Ski Club and others sponsored both events and jumpers in the 1930s.

FRIENDS OF TIMBERLINE COLLECTION

Patch used by Associated Women's Skiers, an all women's ski club from the 1940s.

SIMMONS COLLECTION

A 1940s racer practices slalom racing in the Mile Canyon.

FRIENDS OF TIMBERLINE COLLECTION

"We were called skyriders, the big-hill jumpers. We jumped over 250 feet," says Pletsch who competed for the Canadian national team from 1937-40. "In practice jumps, we might do over 300 feet."

Women also cross-country raced and jumped. A Canadian woman, Isabel Coursier of Revelstoke held the Women's World Champion Ski Jumper title from 1922-29 for jumping 84 feet.

"It has been the general opinion that a lady was a feminine person who kept her head up and her feet down and who always was dignified," wrote Vera Nelson in Cascade's 1931-32 yearbook. "Such a description cannot apply to a lady who skis. Why let the men walk away with all the glory and trophies? ... You are welcome to use any of the jumps as your courage and skill grow. Some girls tried jumping last year. They found it thrilling."

Nelson didn't just talk about jumping, she tried it, according to her daughter, Betty Schuld.

"There was quite a group of young ladies in the Cascade Ski Club in the early thirties," says Schuld. "They were pretty fearless when it came to physical activities. I do recall her talking about going off the 'B' jump at Multorpor." Adds Schuld wryly, "I do not recall anything being said about the landings."

Serviceable landings meant jumpers did not crash upon impact — a disqualifying wallop. Other rules forbade downhill races. The Fédération Internationale de Ski (FIS), skiing's international controlling organization, didn't recognize slalom and downhill racing.

Jumping *was* skiing in the 1920s and 30s. By the 1940s, Austrians' Arlberg ski technique became the Prometheus, stealing fire from the jumpers. More people could learn the snowplow — and the yodel — than the jump.

The British invented the first downhill and slalom races. The most famous, The Roberts of Kandahar Challenge Cup, began in 1911 in Montana, Switzerland. In 1922, Arnold Lunn challenged friends to a gated course pitting speed against turning skill, thus inventing the slalom.

One of the longest continually running races in North American history is the Golden Rose, inaugurated in 1936 by the Oregon Winter Sports Association and held on Mt. Hood. Cascade skiers Boyd French, Jr. and Hvam won it

Early 1930s slalom race at Multorpor.

the first two years. Gretchen Fraser (who later won America's first Olympic gold medal for skiing) won the first women's division in 1938, followed by Cascade's Maryanne Hill in second place.

"I started racing in 1934," says Hill. "My dad cut off a pair of big skis and scraped them down with a piece of glass to make them work. That was my first pair of skis. Cascade Ski Club people took me over to Multorpor and taught me to ski gates. They'd carry my skis up to the top of the course."

At 18, Hill won the 1940 Golden Rose. "I had six-foot, nine-inch Northland skis, and they were terribly heavy," she recalls. "You had to use the same pair of skis for downhill and slalom."

Seven years later, Hill was Oregon's Olympic hopeful with several trophies on her mantel. Tragically, she broke a leg before the trials.

"I was three weeks out of a cast at the 1947 Olympic Trials in Sun Valley," she says. "I finished 17th or 19th."

One of the most prestigious events in Mt. Hood's racing history was one of its earliest. In April 1939, Mt. Hood hosted the National Amateur and Open Downhill and Slalom Ski Championships. The break-neck course ran from

White Stag race flag.

Illumination Rock at 10,000 feet dropping down to 5,490 feet: "The Mt. Hood Turtle-Neck Course."

"The race conditions for the most part were not good for a downhill," recalls Olympian Dick Durrance, who won four of the 12 trophies. "It was fresh, sloppy snow. They used a snowcat to pack, but it was not a wide track. There were no gates, just the top and bottom with one steep pitch but otherwise pretty simple. Nobody fell in love with the course."

If racers fought the slush above Timberline, they respected the hard pack of the slalom down below.

A "flying kilometer" slalom, as titled in the race program, challenged the nation's top skiers at the Tom, Dick and Harry Ski Bowl, a course that Durrance once described as "naked!"

"We had good weather and a good crowd," recalls Durrance who perfected his "Dipsy Doodle" ski turn on wood skis waxed with Bilgiri mittel, a soft wax. Like most racers, he used toe irons, beartrap bindings with long thongs wrapped around his boots. "The slalom was in better shape than the downhill because it had been skied on and packed down."

Internationally celebrated racers Toni Matt, Friedl Pfeifer, Gretchen Fraser and Grace Carter Lindley joined local

heroes Olaf Rodegard, Ariel Edmiston, and Boyd French. They raced for placement on the U.S. Ski Team bound for the Olympics. Unfortunately for the winners, Olympic glory was canceled for World War II.

Meanwhile, Cascade Ski Club immortalized the father of the modern ski race: the annual Arnold Lunn Downhill. The Englishman first visited Mt. Hood in 1937, and returned 25 years later to dedicate the second Magic Mile chairlift.

During his speech, Lunn reportedly called racers of the day a "bunch of ballet dancers on skis," and campaigned to "open up" slalom courses for more of a challenge. He proposed that racers not view courses prior to running the gates.

"The trouble with skiing today," Lunn complained, "is that no one under the age of 70 has any imagination."

Golden Rose, Northwest Ski Championships, Cascade Ski Championships and other traditions offered slaloms and down-mountain events, but for Mt. Hood, racing renown reigned in the summer.

Richard Kohnstamm's greatest contribution to the mountain economy, the lodge's financial stability, ski research and development and racing's fruition was the advent of Summer Racing School and summer skiing in 1956.

"Warren Miller shot an instructional movie above the lodge my first summer, 1955," says Kohnstamm. "He told us how great the skiing was. Warren put a bug in my hat to begin summer skiing.

"I had been to Europe and saw the glacier skiing, but the Americans were not interested in summer racing. The Americans said 'no' to summer skiing and instead wanted to relax and get on the green. The French had summer skiing — and they unabashedly said, 'We are better racers because we have summer skiing.' So we went for it."

During that first solstice, high on the Palmer snowfield and higher at 10,000 feet, under Illumination Saddle and Crater Rock, skiers coated noses with

ACKROYD PHOTO

At left: **Warren Miller, a young cinematographer, came to Timberline in the summer of 1955 to film Aspen's Fred Iselin for an instructional ski movie. Miller, the quintessential ski bum, skied the natural bumps and hillocks of Palmer snowfield.**

Below: **Timberline's first Summer Racing School in 1956 included top racers and coaches from Europe and the states including Robin Miller, Pepi Gabl, Ralph Miller, Penny Pitou, Spence Eckles, Sally Deaver, Duie Davidson, Tom Corcoran, Bea Jordan, Ulla Neilson and Lynn Pearson.**

FRIENDS OF TIMBERLINE COLLECTION, MACONE PHOTO

white, gooey Labiosan and skis with Toko yellow or Metro silver paraffin wax. Olympians and Austrian coaches met racers on Illumination Saddle.

"We made big wonderful giant slalom turns on the snowfield," recalls Olympian Penny Pitou of the summer of 1956. "I'd been racing all winter in Europe with the Olympic team. Dick Kohnstamm came to Cortina, Italy, (the '56 Olympic site) and asked me to be at his first race camp. He said he'd pay round-trip transportation. Round-trip on a Greyhound.

"I graduated from high school, and the next day my parents loaded me on a bus in Boston for the four-day trip. When I got to Portland, Dick wasn't there to pick me up. I called Timberline and he said, 'Oh, you're here today? I'll be down in six hours.'"

If the first summer camp operated on a Greyhound budget, the lift equipment was created on a hitchhiker's pocket change.

"We tried everything up there," recalls John West. "I made a rope tow with a snowcat engine. I got seats from grammar-school desks. You could speed it up, shift gears and slow it down before they got to the top. We had portable pomas, rope tows, handle tows, you name it."

The few dozen skiers and coaches loaded into Tucker Sno-Cats and rode

One of America's longest continually running races, the Golden Rose Race, began in 1936.

FRIENDS OF TIMBERLINE COLLECTION

two miles to the training site.

Timberline's Public Relations man, John Macone, lured racer and Austrian ski star Pepi Gabl to Timberline for the first summer in 1956. Gabl ran the ski school for five years.

Summer Racing School attracted racing's elite to coach: Anderl Molterer, Tony Spiese, Carl Schranz and Ernst Hinterseer, Austrian champions. Campers paid $195 a week for room, board, lift and Sno-Cat privileges, coaching sessions and graduation banquet.

"Pepi Gabl was the head Austrian instructor," says Erich Sailer who runs his own summer race program on Palmer. "He taught what the best World Cup racers were doing. He had some of the top racers for coaches like Ernst Hinterseer, an Austrian who won the 1960 Olympic slalom at Squaw Valley."

A powerful force in skiing worldwide, the Austrians wanted more sovereignty.

"They went on strike one summer," says Kohnstamm "They said, 'We're running this program. We'll dictate how much money you give us.' I kicked them out, fired them!"

The time was ripe for North Americans to replace Europeans. Canadian Ski Team downhiller Lorne O'Connor took over.

"On my first trip to Timberline, I aspired to get on the Canadian National

Kaare Neilson prepares skis for the ride to 10,000 feet and the Summer Racing School.

DEDICATION DAY
PALMER CHAIRLIFT
MT. HOOD

Team," recalls O'Connor, who won the Golden Rose and made the Canadian team in 1957-61. "I went to Hood to race. I stayed on with Summer Racing School in '58 as a chaperone in the dorms.

"I had some really good experiences as a result of Dick Kohnstamm's generosity, being exposed to quality coaches in his racing school. Dick always had quality people like Adrien Duvillard from France and Pepi Stiegler. I was a chaperone and a ski racer. You had all young kids in dorms who needed chaperones because after lights out, they'd wreck the place."

Camps grew but not until installation of the Palmer Chairlift in 1979 did the snowfield draw international attention.

"It was pretty primitive compared to today," says Hank Tauber, former U.S. Ski Team coach. "We'd go up in the morning in huge cats, 15 to 20 people. It was a little dicey coming downhill (in the machines), but the run out was long enough that we didn't worry too much. The portable lifts had to be adjusted as the snow melted. We had two platter pulls end to end."

Tauber's Timberline Summer Racing Camp drew 200 to 300 kids from across the continent. Aside from a camp near Red Lodge, Montana, Timberline's was the only annual racing program although both Oregon's Mt. Bachelor and California's Mammoth Mountain occasionally offered summer sessions.

"I approached Kohnstamm about lift-served skiing on Palmer," says Tauber. "I thought that there was enough of a skiing population to sustain a summer lift."

"Summer skiing was rinky dink with pomas," admits Kohnstamm. "Hank said, 'You're doing this all wrong. You need a chairlift.' So we built it. Look now — nowhere else in North America has skiing year-round."

The grand experiment wasn't without challenges specific to Mt. Hood.

Skiers load at the midway station on Palmer. Summer skiing evolved from snowcats and hiking in 1956 to baby pomas in 1967, then the Palmer double chairlift in 1979, and finally the Palmer Express quad chairlift installed in 1997.

"Palmer blew down the first winter," recalls Kohnstamm. "We had to rebuild it with supporting tripods on the towers."

Another summer, national teams from Japan, America and Europe canceled training after news reports falsely stated that the mountain was destined to blow. Geologists studying volcanic activity recorded what they thought were over 50 tremors one day. The media reported that the sleeping volcano would erupt. Coincidentally, neighbor Mt. Hood Meadows had dynamited the same number of tree stumps!

Mt. Hood's few erroneous moments in the limelight paled to a local kid's fame. After decades of the Europeans' medal monarchy, Mt. Hood finally hit paydirt with downhiller Bill Johnson. He purloined the 1984 Olympic downhill gold medal away from the Europeans.

"Hood's a great place to grow up," says Johnson. "We went into the Cascade Ski Club race program because (Coach) Rene Farwig had yet to set up a program on the other side of the mountain. At that time,

"Lynn Pearson and I started the Turkey Slalom Race at Thanksgiving," says Joie Smith. "The winner won a live turkey. It was quite an ordeal to handle the bird."

P Gabl

E Sailer

"We taught the New Austrian technique," says Erich Sailer who coached under Pepi Gabl. "It used big angulation. The main ingredient of the technique was unnatural, extreme angulation — very bad for your body. Austrian and French techniques stemmed from racing. I learned from Pepi to look at racers then take advantage of their successful techniques and put those techniques into skiing."

the French were the hottest on the tour. In 1968 Jean Claude Killy won a few golds. The French team was so stacked that B Team members couldn't get on the French team, so Rene got them to coach in the U.S."

By the time Johnson turned 14, he beat 18-year-olds.

"Toni Leuthold and I were beating all the older kids," he recalls. "The French coaches influenced my racing, but really,

your destiny is your destiny. No matter who's coaching, you have to make it down the mountain yourself."

That he did, racing with the U.S. Ski Team for a decade.

"I can ski but I'm not a great athlete," Johnson told guests at Cascade Ski Club's 50th Anniversary party in 1996. "I won the Europa Cup title and the downhill title. I was the first American to do that. I told the other racers at Sarajevo (Olympics), 'I don't know why you're here. I wouldn't want to race for second place!'"

While racing's best from North America, Japan, and Europe train on Palmer's summer slopes, local races challenge youngsters. Mt. Hood Race Team (now combined with Mt. Hood Ski Academy), high schools, and other groups sponsor teams and events.

The nation's largest high school alpine ski competition, the Christine Cato Memorial Race, is held every January. The slalom race commemorates a high-school athlete who died on the mountain.

"We have 485 kids racing from two large high school leagues," says Judy Cato, who organizes each season's premier event. "It's run on Christine's Course on 'The Mile' unless the weather sends us to Victoria Station."

Olympian and Austrian Ski Team racer Putzi Frandl joined the Summer Racing School in 1958. Many famous skiers coached or trained on Mt. Hood's southern slope including Ernst Hinterseer, Toni Sailer, Karl Schranz, Roger Staub, Billy Kidd, Suzy Chaffee, Phil and Steve Mahre, Jan Bucher, Jimmy Heuga, Cindy Nelson, Bill Johnson, Billy Koch, Tamara, McKinney, Tommy Moe, A.J. Kitt, Marc Giradelli, Picabo Street, Diane Roffe-Steinrotter and Bonnie St. John.

Cato Memorial Race pin

While ski racers discipline themselves in tight, technical courses, the newcomers, snowboarders, pursue the unconventional.

Snowboarding began with Jake Burton testing his sliding device, the Snurfer, in the late 1960s. The New Yorker started a tsunami that hit the Northwest hard enough to influence more than half the visitors to snow country. On wave's crest is John Ingersoll whose High Cascade Snowboard Camp draws 1,400 youths to Mt. Hood for freestyle aerials, a nose grab and maybe a backside 540.

"I lost my skis, stolen out of my locker at Mt. Bachelor," says former ski racer Ingersoll. "So I haven't skied in five years. I started High Cascade because at the time I was base operations manager for Alpine Ski Camp. Every day I'd pick up snowboarders hitchhiking down the hill. They'd missed their bus, and the camp they attended didn't have an accounting system to know how many kids were on the hill. I thought I could do better."

Between High Cascade and three other camps, 3,300 snowboard campers train at Mt. Hood each summer.

SNOW*boarding Business* magazine's Stuart Craig writes, "Pro riders, product managers, wannabes, groupies, and of course the campers — all come to Mt. Hood every summer to create the crucible of industry momentum that is arguably hotter than the winter scene." He quotes industry marketers as pointing out that whatever happens in the snowboard industry, happens first at Mt. Hood.

"One guy saw snowboarding as pushing skiers out of Government Camp,"

The evolution of ski boots from leather to plastics altered preparation rituals. "In 1947 my first pair of boots, skis and poles cost $47," says Duane Bridge. "We all had Molitor boots. To break them in, we'd use a bathtub full of half alcohol, half water. We'd fill up the boots and stand in them for two or three hours. We'd take them off and hope they were molded to our feet."

At right: Swiss Champion Roger Staub is framed by a Mt. Hood racer.

At left: Leather ski boots dry in the summer sun near the Timberline Pool, early 1960s.

FRIENDS OF TIMBERLINE COLLECTION

Ingersoll adds. "He was short sighted. We are not pushing skiers out but going with a change of the times."

Summer snow will continue to draw more snowboarders and new tricks. Ingersoll predicts more precision from competition-bound boarders.

"If you watch half-pipe contests, they land on top of a transition or crash on the deck or land flat and stop," observes Ingersoll. "You watch the spinning; it's not clean. The tricks are not smooth. So in two or three Olympics, snowboarding will become more like ice skating with really clean spins and much tighter competition than there is now."

Hundreds of spectators line the half

pipes, reminiscent of the 1930s and ski jumping. The big-air artists dish up mid-air antics while wearing clothes that mimic the fluttering baggies of Dick Durrance's 1939 nationals.

"Snowboarders have a lot of fun," chuckles octogenarian Durrance. "I wish I were young enough to try it!"

Like an oracle, the training lanes of the Palmer snowfield reveal a high-speed vision of the future. Adjacent to the snowboarders are the alpine racers, telemarkers, mogul bashers, ballet skiers and aerial freestylists. In a climate of innovation and inspiration, snowsports' legacy and future are cultivated on the summer snowfields of Mt. Hood. ⎯⎯

Adult ski racing leagues challenge teams from around the mountain.

High Cascade Snowboard Camp is one of several summer camps that attract thousands of youngsters like Stephen Scott to half pipes and terrain gardens on the mountain. Palmer is training ground to well-known boarders like Ross Powers, Mike Jacoby, Jeanie Waara, Lisa Kosglow, Sondra Van Ert, Chris Engelsman and local kid Josh Linn.

Chris Simbo freestyling.

Akjas and Splints

MHSP members wore armbands to identify themselves on the slopes. "We took them off before entering the Blue Ox Bar," says a patrol member.

Opposite page: Transporting a victim are members of the Mt. Hood Ski Patrol including Joe Leuthold, second from the left, and Hank Lewis, second from the right. Circa 1938.

"In the early years of skiing...the untracked wastes of powdery snow were visited only by a few hardy souls who walked approximately four miles uphill and with the aid of much effort reached timberline," wrote District Ranger, Ralph Wiese, of the early 1930s in the 1940 *Annual of the Wy'east Climbers.* "There were very few accidents and if a person was injured his friends would do some improvising and eventually would get the victim out."

Skiing's popularity drew thousands to the mountains although some came unprepared and unschooled. A 1936 newspaper reported, "Snow ambulance ready. Camp Blossom gets sled for accident aid. Stationed now at the old timberline cabin, long known as Camp Blossom, is the Timberline Taxi. The sled was donated by Mrs. Ray Walker of Portland and two mattresses that were hauled were donated by (Mrs. Alex) Negoescus.'"

Broken legs and twisted ankles, lost skiers and frozen kids spurred the Wy'east Climbers and the Nile River Yacht Club to approach the USFS with

Joe Leuthold's Mt. Hood Ski Patrol pin. The original 50 patrol members drew for their patrol numbers. The pin's shape is derived from the USFS shield. MHSP is the only patrol in the nation allowed to use the forest service emblem likeness.

LEUTHOLD COLLECTION

At right: On one of their first searches, MHSP members prepare to probe snow for the tracks of a lost skier/climber in January 1938. "The Mazamas counted noses and came up one nose short," recalls Hank Lewis. "A fellow named Russell Guffroy was missing. We had 100 people up there after the storm cleared. We set up a grid from above the lodge to where Silcox Hut is now and swept across the slope. We found his skis but not Guffroy."

an unprecedented proposal. In November 1937, they asked for USFS to support a patrol on skis. Barney MacNab and Everett Darr suggested to the USFS that an official patrol for the trails down the mountain from Timberline was necessary.

They told the District Ranger, Harold Engles, "We know a guy we can put up to the job, a guy capable of creating a ski patrol." The guy was fellow climber and Wy'easter, Hank Lewis.

"The upshot was, I could get away on weekends," says Lewis. "I worked in a filling station. Harold Engles hung a tin buzzer on me that read, 'Forest Guard.'

He said, 'Start a ski patrol.' I said that I didn't know. I needed equipment. I went down to the Wy'east cabin and dug out the toboggan. I tapped guys to be in the patrol. We had arm bands and that was the ski patrol."

While the USFS paid Lewis $10 a weekend to patrol, he and a group of volunteers formed the Mt. Hood Ski Patrol. On March 2, 1938, 50 members elected Lewis as the first patrol chief and MacNab as president. As the nation's premier volunteer patrol, the Oregonians pioneered rescue methodology and provided a vanguard for future volunteer and professional patrols to copy.

Photos from that era show a dozen

CALDWELL PHOTO

men hamming it up during their first-aid course in a Portland basement. Yet patrolling demanded precision and expertise in mountain travel and rescue. The volunteers took their job seriously.

"We learned early that anytime we had a search, the first thing to do was to check all the bars," says Lewis.

"If a kid was missing, like a group of Boy Scouts missing a boy, we soon learned to call his home because he'd gotten a ride with one of his buddies."

Those were happy endings. Unfortunately, some unhappy endings occurred.

"For me this was a very sad experience," says Willis Caldwell. "It was a ski patrol search in 1938 for a lost skier. Everything went wrong (for the skiers) that could have gone wrong. Two men died. One might have had a heart attack and the other died from exposure. Patrol members used bamboo poles to probe for foot prints of the skier who had lost his way in a blizzard and had taken off his skis. He had walked on snow with a breakable crust covered with eight inches of fresh powdered snow."

Several factors contribute to tragedies in the early ski days and today: lack of adequate equipment and clothing; lack of skiing or climbing expertise; and lack of common sense.

The foremost challenge to lost or injured skiers remains the perilous and unpredictable weather brewed by Oregon's highest peak. White-outs, blizzards and ice storms boil in with little warning, leaving recreationalists with no visibility.

Such rescues or body-retrieval missions caught headlines across the nation and sometimes around the globe. Often, the rescuers risked their own lives and received little thanks.

"One time we found a young boy who had been lost above the lodge," Lewis says. "When we brought him to the waiting arms of his family, all they could say to us was 'Who stole his mitten?'"

Meanwhile, on the other side of the continent, another ski patrol formed. Also in 1938, members of the Amateur Ski Club of New York organized a volunteer ski patrol for the National Downhill Races at Stowe, Vermont. So impressed with the patrol was Roger Langley, National Ski Association president, that he asked the patrol organizer Charles "Minnie" Dole to create a national patrol.

CALDWELL PHOTO

"Three feet of snow had fallen the night of the storm, so we dug down and found footsteps frozen under the fresh snow," says Hank Lewis. "We probed with ski poles, then probed with slalom poles wrapped with cotton and gauze so there was an end on it like a ski pole. We tracked into Sand Canyon, probed across and finally found Guffroy frozen to death, sitting upright, slumped over slightly and under some trees."

Some people dispute MHSP's claim as the first organized patrol in America. In actuality, America's first National Park, Yellowstone, had America's first ski patrol! Its purpose was decidedly different from rescuing injured skiers: April 1887 saw Yellowstone ski patrol's first arrest of a poacher in possession of beaver and otter furs as reported by writer T.E. Hofer in *Forest and Stream* magazine, May 5, 1887.

LEUTHOLD COLLECTION

"It was late 1938 that Langley and Dole came to Mt. Hood to look over our organization," recalls Caldwell. "They liked what they saw and designed the National Ski Patrol (NSP) after the Mt. Hood Patrol."

Eventually the patrols merged only to separate, citing liability insurance mandates and financial disputes.

From the beginning, Ralph Wiese kept detailed records for the USFS on skier accidents and discovered that 70 percent of all the accidents occurred with first year novices. Second-year skiers accrued 28 percent of the accidents.

Most accidents victims were first year novices according to USFS District Ranger Ralph Wiese.

Wiese wrote, that of the 24,404 skiers on the south side of Mt. Hood skiing in January 1939, 146 accidents were reported. That winter drew 89,810 skier visits with a total of 420 accidents November through March. "We concluded that the way to reduce accidents was to have a ski school," says Lewis.

The unprecedented free ski school at Summit soon outgrew the patrol's capabilities. The Portland Jaycees took over the school while patrollers returned to their toboggans and splints.

"We used to cook up pretty fancy ideas over beer," says Lewis.

One of those fancy ideas, developed in the basement of MHSP's patrol chief Harold Johnson. In 1949, Johnson created a light-weight box splint of plywood and cravats with foam padding. One of the best asides to the Johnson Splint was its light weight: it could be sent back from the hospital by mail — just a few stamps glued to its side.

Still in use today, the Johnson Splint, or versions of it, became *de rigeur* with patrols around the Northwest.

Early toboggans, called "dog sleds" and "snub noses," did the job although some patrollers considered them "ghastly wooden things," that outweighed some patrollers.

In 1958, MHSP imported a contraption that proved its worth, the *akja*, a

Ski Patrol line up roll call April 1, 1939.

"Finnish Snowboat." The sled immediately improved the transportation of victims. Once again, other patrols around the country saw merit in MHSP's *akjas* and bought their own.

Northwesterners again led the country with possibly the first all-women ski patrol in the world. Both the MHSP and NSP rosters listed only men until 1946; however, wives and girlfriends shared safeguard duties.

"They called themselves the Stormy Petrels after the birds in the Arctic," says Lewis. "They were never formally part of the patrol, but they went to first aid and took all the classes."

"We got tired of hearing the fellows talk about patrol, so we formed the Stormy Petrels," recalls Marian Dukehart. "The men took a course in first aid and the women did too — some could have been certified ski patrol people in the 1930s, when Timberline Lodge was being built."

Dukehart, Maggey Latta, Katie Mac-Nab Patton, Fran Markewitz, Harriet Givens and others assisted at accident sites.

"I can remember when I became a good enough skier to be trusted to ski down with the eggs," laughs Dukehart, explaining that before Timberline Road existed, skiers packed food in — and leftovers out.

When war drew many MHSP mem-

NELSON-SCHULD COLLECTION

bers to foreign soil, women sidestepped onto the patrol. They joined the cultural change overtaking the country and proved that women had both the physical strength and fortitude for rescue work. In the latter 1940s, more than a dozen women wore MHSP badges. One of the women, Laurita Leuthold, joined her husband on rescues.

"A group from Chicago had come to climb the mountain," says Leuthold. "On the descent, somebody slipped and the whole works went down into a bergschrund. The kid on the bottom died. The USFS asked my husband, Joe, to help. There were numerous injuries. It was dark. Joe and I were in charge of one

"I was one of five women on the 1960 Olympic patrol." A successful racer herself, Joie Smith (pictured at right) raced in the 1951 U.S. Nationals. Her Olympic aspirations were crushed in a bad fall in the 1955 Golden Rose Race. The downhill racer in front of her fell on the narrow and salted course. To avoid hitting the downed skier and people assisting at the accident site, Smith had to ski out of the course into soft snow where she crashed and broke her leg in 30 places. A visible force on the mountain, she ran the ski shop at Timberline in 1953-54, and then opened her own ski shop in Rhododendron in 1954. She closed it in 1968 when she started her Alpine Towing, dealing with "the unpleasant side of skiing."

Squaw Olympics logo.

SMITH COLLECTION

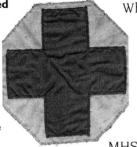

toboggan. It was icy and slippery. We had more than six people handling each sled because of the conditions. When they saw I was in the group, some of the guys objected because I was a female. They calmed down when they realized that Joe and I were the only two with headlamps."

Betty Nelson Schuld joined MHSP in 1946 as one of the first woman to officially join aside from Ethyl Fullman who ran the patrol's first aid

At right: MHSP patrolman and lift operator load a toboggan on the Magic Mile chairlift. "I recall that it was rather a chancy trip to pick up someone with the old toboggans," says Ken Arthur, early MHSP member. "I don't think we ever lost anybody in a toboggan though."

NELSON-SCHULD COLLECTION

room. The three trails to Government Camp gave the patrol several miles to safeguard. Schuld recalls:

"One evening a girl friend and I were heading down the trail. A call came that there was a man about a mile down with a broken leg. The two of us were put into service. We arrived at the accident scene and found a man in a lot of discomfort and shock. He also weighed about 250 pounds, 30 pounds more than the two of us together! On top of that, the toboggan probably weighed 80 pounds. The trail was not all down hill, some flat and some uphill. We'd left Timberline about 4 p.m. and reached the first aid office in Government Camp about 8 p.m."

Mt. Hood's northern slopes were not excluded from mishaps. According to Bill Pattison, patrolling on the north side started with several Crag Rats, a mountain-climbing club, whose members joined the MHSP.

"We were invited into the ski patrol through Dick Pooley who said, 'Hey, I've got good sled handlers here with training.' Most were ambulance drivers or firemen who had Emergency Medical Training," recalls Pattison.

So the Crag Rats, known for their checkered shirts, put on new uniforms, the rust-colored patrol parkas and the shield of MHSP on the left breast. When

Mt. Hood Meadows opened in 1968, the Hood River volunteers spent weekends at the new area.

"That first year we were only open weekends and holidays so the volunteers covered the area," recalls Keith Petrie, the first mountain manager at Meadows. "We were working so hard, I didn't notice that we weren't operating every day."

The following year three pro-patrollers worked midweek. Volunteers patrolled on weekends.

When a report went out that a child was lost, every employee became part of the search, recalls Meadow's Jodi Gehrman:

"I'd never been involved in a rescue, but I wound up dispatcher," she recalls. "Two separate groups were lost, a young brother and sister and another group. All the management, ski school, patrol, everybody was involved. All were found ok. I'll never forget the letter we got from the kids' father. 'We love Mt. Hood but that night that mountain looked like a big white tomb. Thank you,' they said, 'for restoring our wonderful image of Mt. Hood!'"

With the growing popularity of skiing, need arose for ski patrollers beyond weekends. Professional ski patrols appeared on the national level before WWII in Sun Valley and as early as 1947 in a few ski areas such as Aspen. Organized patrols were an American phenomenon, says Olympian Dick Durrance.

"When I lived in Europe (1920s and 30s) there were no patrols," he recalls. "If you were hurt, ski instructors might haul you out, but you'd pay for the service."

On Mt. Hood, skiing minister Jim McGugin gave sermons on Sundays and first aid the rest of the week.

"Almost every year I had an employee on patrol with me," recalls McGugin of the early 1960s. "We had night skiing so we had to have two patrollers. I started out at $600 a month — not a bad salary with the room and board."

His wife, Evelyn, designed and sewed the patrol's patch, "the colors of the lodge, yellow with a red cross in the middle," he says.

When McGugin quit in the spring of 1965, Gretchen Dauelsberg (McMillin) got the job at $1.40 an hour.

"I'd flag danger areas like around the lodge where someone could fall between the lodge and a snowbank," she

MHSP's first *akjas* cost $88 each and were imported from Austria, recalls Keith Petrie. "The Bavarian Red Cross used them," he says. "The *akja* was used in the Russian-Finnish War. The Finns held the Russians to a standstill because they were able to move equipment on the *akjas* while the Russians were buried in the deep snow."

TALSMA PHOTO

recalls. "I'd put ropes up. Mostly I'd sit in a lift shack with the lift crew and wait. I never really had more than one accident case a week. On the Mile somebody spiral-fractured a leg. I had to get him off the mountain. I put him in an *akja*. The Mile was wind packed and drifted, and I couldn't pop off the drifts with a badly injured skier. I walked, pulling the *akja*. They didn't groom much in those days."

Although the *akjas* refined rescue procedure, by the late 1970s, new plastics, ski technology and snow grooming pushed patrolling into the next evolutionary step. Victor Bradley made a fiberglass sled he called the Cascade which lightened a patroller's load by 30 pounds.

"He got tired of pulling old wooden Sun Valleys, the sleds up at Stevens Pass," says Victor's son Bob Bradley who now manufacturers the sleds. "He thought there had to be a better way, so he constructed a toboggan out of one piece of fiberglass like a boat."

Bradley's first Cascade sold for about $150 in 1962. Since then Bradleys have shipped over 10,000 Cascade sleds around the world.

"The *akjas* were primitive and required high maintenance," says Dale Crockatt who became Timberline Patrol Director in 1978. "The MHSP volunteers had lots of money involved in the *akjas*. The Cascade was only $300 and was a one-man sled, lighter and more maneuverable in some conditions."

Crockatt's biggest challenge came not from bandages but from bumper-to-bumper climbers scaling Hood. Palmer chairlift's 1977 construction lay along the busiest route up the peak. Grooming machines packed the snow and allowed climbers an easier march. Yet some climbers left more than their footprints.

"It became a civil war," says Crockatt. "We tried to get the skiers and climbers to realize that they were the same people — mountain lovers. Snow Ranger Bruce Haynes and I got the idea to make a trail from the parking lot next to White River Canyon so the climbers would stay off the groomed runs. It worked."

Seattle skier Victor Bradley invented a lighter, more maneuverable rescue sled he called the Cascade.

KOHNSTAMM COLLECTION

TALSMA PHOTO

Tobogganing

Rescue sleds hauled injured skiers and climbers, and other cargo. In Government Camp, toboggan passengers paid a few cents to scream down a toboggan run behind the Battle Axe Inn during the late 1920s and 30s.

"We had a toboggan run in connection with our business," recalls Marcella Villiger King of a time when 15 cents bought a burger. "We had long toboggans that were pulled uphill with an electrical tow. We had our own power plant for the Inn. The first rescuers used our toboggans too. It was the only equipment available to move a body."

One of the early rope tows on Mt. Hood was made by Sweden Freezers, a Seattle company that manufactured ice cream dispensing machines.

"It had a gas-powered engine," recalls Hank Lewis. "The engine was bolted on to a six-foot toboggan and set up with a half-inch rope and pulley to walk its way up the hill. Then we anchored the engine at the top."

Some Mt. Hood sleds traveled. For the 1960 Olympics, Joie Smith volunteered to patrol at Squaw Valley. With her went six *akjas* to assist in patrolling the Olympics.

"It was a transitory period when the NSP was changing from dog sleds to *akjas*," she recalls. "I used one of the *akjas* on a crash on the giant slalom course."

Years later when ski patrol supervisor Darrel Winterborne was asked if an employee could patrol using telemark skis, Winterborne challenged telemarker Jamie Priestly.

"I had to prove I could handle a large person on the sled while I telemarked," says Priestly of the 1980s. "So Darrel sat on the sled while I telemarked. No problem."

While patrollers most often use toboggans for serious business, thieves once pilfered a sled to steal a keg of beer.

"Whoever stole the keg, eventually returned it and the sled," says Patrol Supervisor, Janie Swift. "Empty of course."

LEUTHOLD COLLECTION

Joe Leuthold inspects the first aid toboggan. "The original toboggan had a chain on the front to use as a braking device," recalls Raymond Conkling. "You'd throw the chain under the sled to slow it down. That sled fell into disuse when MHSP acquired the 'dog sled' that had a handle on the front and rear of the toboggan. We called it a 'dog sled' because the person controlling the sled in the front looked like a dog, bending over the sled like that."

With the advent of chairlift-accessed summer skiing came hundreds of skiers, racers and new first-aid concerns. Palmer opened the summer of 1979 and with it a different kind of incident. A bikini-clad skier might lose a little flesh on the snow, or a vicious sunburned nose needed attention.

But it was the racers who loved the hard, smooth early morning surface and high speed that concerned them the most.

Fortunately for Mt. Hood's first woman patrol director, the most memorable of her job's duties were early mornings at the top of Palmer.

"About 5:30 a.m., we'd take a cat to the top to open the lift," says Janie Swift, Timberline's patrol leader 1988-90. "We'd break through clouds, a colorful blanket with the rising sun. The mountain formed a pyramid shadow over the Willamette Valley on the clouds below us."

Swift and her crew broadcast rock salt by hand each morning to force the top layer of snow to freeze to the next layer. They realigned signs and flags to keep skiers from wandering. And they barbecued.

"Bob Albright, a maintenance guy, made eggs Benedict in the morning," laughs Swift. "On the last day of summer, we had a big barbecue on Palmer. Rick Hower brought fresh salmon and

after the last skier went down, 60 or 70 people would hang around the top of Palmer, sometimes until the next day. Somebody always brought a battery-operated blender."

Thus went the luxurious days of summer, occasionally impeded by climbing rescues and ski wrecks.

"Patrol work was a lot of babysitting the skiers," admits Swift, now an emergency room nurse. "For most patrollers and rescuers, there will be an incident that affects them more than all others, an accident or search with such far-reaching effects that people will quit the organization. When a child dies, something inside all of us dies. I know a lot of people never get past that."

Despite a few notorious incidents on Mt. Hood, the number of accidents remains below the national average of 3.4 per thousand skiers.

"Prevention became important," says Renee Lamoreau Tripp who patrolled 1987-96. "We look at hazards and realize what needs to be marked. We don't see as many boot-top fractures as we used to." Current Patrol Director Jim Tripp agrees.

"Although we see that snowboarders and skiers are injured at about the same rate, the injuries have changed," says Tripp. "We see more wrist injuries with snowboarders and air-oriented injuries."

As the method of sliding over snow evolves, so does ski patrolling. From meetings in a Portland basement in 1937 to a worldwide profession, Mt. Hood rescuers remain on the cutting edge utilizing Mountain Locater Units (MLU), the first in the world. The electronic devices, in service since 1988, work like wildlife tracking transmitters.

"After the Oregon Episcopal School climbing accident in 1986 where nine kids died on the mountain, we decided there was a need for backcountry transmitters," says Scott Russell of the Mountain Signal Memorial Fund. "The MHSP had proposed a similar kind of system 12 years earlier but couldn't get anybody to handle it because of liability issues."

Rescue organizations successfully petitioned Oregon's legislature to exempt the MLU manufacturer from tort claims involving the device.

"Transmitters are rented by climbers and turned on only if the climbers feel they are in danger," says Portland Mountain Rescue volunteer Rocky Henderson. "This is the only place in America where the MLUs are used because of the legal hoops involved."

Rescue efforts are often based at Timberline and include trained search and rescue groups from Clackamas and Hood River County Sheriffs' offices, the Crag Rats and Timberline Lodge employees. Receivers pick up the climbers' signal.

"We've had neat successes finding people who get lost in a white out where you don't know up from down," adds Russell.

Ralph Wiese's "untracked wastes of powdery snow" in the 1930s are no more or less dangerous after a hundred years of skiing. Innovations from these hardworking mountaineers reverberate nationwide, their lessons educate the public, and their efforts lessen the grasp of tragedy. ᗧᗞ

Mt. Hood Ski Patrol Pin, 50 Years, 1937-1987. NSP currently lists 27,000 members worldwide, including the MHSP's 290 constituents who remain loyal to skiers in the Northwest.

KOHNSTAMM COLLECTION

KOHNSTAMM COLLECTION

Ski jumping WAS skiing.

Downhill skiing was for sissies!

— Otto Lang

Skiers schussed Oregon's slopes at the turn of the century, yet it wasn't until 1938 that the first professional ski school opened on Mt. Hood. Meanwhile, the Cascade Ski Club had offered Sunday lessons since 1931. The club's advice transcends the ages.

"Don't use the highway and parking spaces for skiing and sledding," wrote Myron E. Jones in Cascade's yearbook *The Take-Off*. "Don't mistake courage for ability and exceed your capacity. Don't expect your skis to go the way you're looking. Start early on tournament days and return late to help relieve the traffic congestion."

Austrian Otto Lang, famous for his 1936 book *Downhill Skiing*, explained ski technique for his readers and students and glamorized the unfledged sport.

"Quite a coterie of Norwegian ski jumpers competed in the Northwest in the 1930s," recalls Lang. "Ski jumping *was* skiing. Downhill skiing was for sissies! The Norwegians treated me haugh-

MACONE PHOTO

tily. I'd been a jumper in my younger years but was out of practice. I opened a jump hill and all of a sudden they had a different attitude, became courteous.

"Some big shots of the time said they would like to take lessons and polish up on their skiing. They were confident. I told them, 'When it comes to downhill, you don't know the mechanics of skiing. So what we do is start from the bottom with the snowplow turn.' Their jaws dropped. Back to the snowplow? But they caught on quickly, you know, because Norwegians are natural-born skiers. We became very good friends."

The Norwegians invented skiing as a sport. They invented jumping. In the 1860s, Norwegians invented turns called the Telemark and the Christiania, named after a Norwegian region and city.

Under Lang's tutelage, Northwesterner Ariel Edmiston ran the teaching at Timberline during the weeks Lang spent piloting his two other ski schools at Mt. Ranier and Mt. Baker.

"I brought Arlberg style based on the snowplow to the U.S.," says Lang, who taught for Hannes Schneider's famous St. Anton school in the Austrian Alps. "The Arlberg style and snowplow are the foundation of the whole alpine technique around the world, even today."

Theirs was a proper era of skiing when instructors wore wool suits and neckties, often Austrian boiled wool jackets with leather lapels. Students might wear Portland-made Hirsch-Weis winter sports togs. Instructors taught the stem turn and the civility of filling in the "bathtubs" — the holes where students crashed.

Betty Cronin Meier relishes the skiing down from the old Timberline Cabin in the early 1930s.

"Before the Arlberg technique of skiing, we just went down the narrow trails as best we could," she says. "Sometimes we sat on our ski poles to slow us down. After the lodge was finished, there still wasn't a lift, so we climbed to Lone Fir Cabin and skied

Karl Molitor and Rosemary Bleuer of the Swiss Olympic Team in 1947, ski at Timberline.

ACKROYD PHOTO

down, making three or four runs a day. Then a few people got together and bought Otto Lang a rope tow. We learned our first snow plows and stem Christianias."

"Nobody knew how to ski back then," says Hank Lewis. "Skiing didn't really take off until Otto Lang got into the act with his book *Downhill Skiing*. Lang trained instructors for the ski patrol. He'd just teach the snowplow. Then he could get more business teaching the next level of skills."

Only one year at Timberline and Otto Lang was lured to Idaho and Sun Valley's star-studded clientele. Other European experts took over the ski school and modified and improved the Arlberg's snowplow, stem christie, and pure christie or parallel swing.

As a handful of students learned proper technique from the pros, hundreds of others skipped the lessons and littered the trails with enough injuries to keep the new Mt. Hood Ski Patrol in bull-market business in 1938.

"When we started the Mt. Hood Ski Patrol, Ralph Wiese kept accurate records on cases we treated," recalls Lewis "Seventy percent of all accident cases were first-year novices. Twenty-eight percent were second year novices."

They inaugurated a free ski school at Multorpor.

"We anticipated 50-60 people, but 500 showed up!" he adds.

Successful yet cumbersome, the school needed more instructors. In stepped the *Oregonian* and *Oregon Journal* newspapers. They oversaw the free ski school while the patrol went back to rescues.

A 1940 ski movie by Timberline's George Henderson captured skiing's bold image. Ski teachers demonstrating the *gelandesprung* jump over cornices while the narrator describes "four hours of class instruction daily, private lessons and special classes in slalom, downhill, jumping and cross-country running."

One of the airborne instructors was Norwegian ski jumper Olaf Rodegard. He traveled the West jumping in ski tournaments, "Canada to California and east to Sun Valley," recalls Rodegard. "Come 1939 I thought it was time to try to make a living out of my skiing. So my good friend Fred Van Dyke (lodge manager) asked me to come up there to teach. That year Prince Olav of Norway opened the Magic Mile by screwing on a gold nut to the lower tower.

"The technique was the old Arlberg follow-through with the arms," says Rodegard. "But then in slalom, we found that in follow-through, you were overturned and not ready for the next turn. So then came that little hop with the

MACONE PHOTO. FRIENDS OF TIMBERLINE COLLECTION.

heels, left, right, left, right, with a little *revörst* shoulder to get the weight on the lower ski. From then on everybody skis alike. Amen."

In June, 1941, Rodegard was drafted. He joined the 10th Mountain Division of ski troops.

Swiss racer Martin Fopp managed Timberline's ski school. His ski style countered Arlberg.

"In the Swiss Technique, the skier used the inside shoulder to lead the turn," says Fopp. "The Arlberg skiers swung the outside shoulder to initiate a turn."

Fopp had ventured to the states to ski race, and went on the take the U.S. National downhill title in 1942. His secret formula: Sohm's red wax and paraffin.

Olaf Rodegard jumping a cornice, circa 1940.

LIDELL PHOTO

"As the war was just declared, there were not too many skiers," says Fopp. "I had a special student at Timberline. She was a wealthy young woman who came to the lodge for the winter with her chauffeur, maid and two dogs. She was quite eccentric. Her lessons were from four to five p.m. She would ski about 100 yards, take off her skis and start throwing snowballs at me. Later, she would have a cake on a chair in the dining room and demanded that I sit upon it!"

Wacky students did not goad Fopp to quit teaching, but WWII forced skiing into a hockey stop. Lifts, lodges and lessons lapsed into a three-year hiatus — at least for the general public.

"When I was drafted, I had the right to come back and take over the ski school again when and if I got back after the war," says Rodegard. "Back I came. I was discharged December 3, 1945, a little late for starting the ski season. So I ordered my second in command, Dick Cochran, who was discharged before me, to start classes the week before Thanksgiving."

Meanwhile, Multorpor put the ski tow back into operation.

"After the war, the Portland Junior Chamber of Commerce set up and charged $1 a lesson, and it went over real big," says Hank Lewis. "They did a lot for

FOPP COLLECTION

skiing to have a low-cost ski school."

By the time alpinists used aluminum instead of bamboo ski poles in the late 1950s, Oregon skiers made 500,000 visits annually to 20 areas including long-forgotten slopes of Arbuckle, Little Alps, Taft Mountain and Tomahawk.

Europeans controlled many ski schools throughout the West. Austrian Erich Sailer ran a modest Timberline Ski School with 25 students on a busy day,

Swiss racer Martin Fopp taught skiing at Timberline in the 1940s. He won the 1938 Parsenn Derby, the longest downhill race in the world, in a record of 13:06 minutes. He obtained his Swiss ski instructor certification in 1930 and taught skiing for 51 years including a stint at Timberline when lessons cost $2 a day, and a week's lodging, meals, lifts and lessons cost $39.50.

Ski School Director Lorne O'Connor teaches Jeff Kohnstamm the Canadian ski technique 1966.

O'CONNOR COLLECTION

teaching the new Austrian technique.

"We taught what the most successful racers skied," says Sailer. "Extreme angulation was main ingredient of the technique. It was unnatural. It was very bad for your body. The techniques stemmed from racing. We looked at racers then took advantage of that and put it in skiing. It's the same in all sports."

In one winter he taught 200 private lessons, more than any instructor before him.

"We had the elite of Portland coming up because Timberline was like a clubhouse, a country club for them in winter," Sailer says. "The private lessons kept the ski school going.

"Everything was difficult at Mt. Hood because of the weather. Many times the Mile lift did not run. We had the Betsy rope tow to use. I had a student from Portland, a big heavy man. He sunk into soft snow up to his neck. It took me two hours to get him out again! There was no way to handle the massive amount of snow. I never forgot that. It was just a little way from the lodge yet no one knew I was struggling to get him out."

Unbeknownst to Sailer and Kohnstamm, some ski areas experimented with machine-packing slopes. It was the next ski school director, Canadian Lorne

Ski fashion after WWII included army-surplus anoraks like Adlai Stevenson (on right) and an administrative aide wore during Stevenson's campaign visit to the Northwest. "Stevenson needed rest from the presidential primaries campaign, so we arranged to have him up at the mountain," recalls John Macone. "We were out in a cat in a bad storm and rode up on a cornice. The cornice collapsed, and we rolled 30 feet down into a canyon. We got out and struggled through the snow to the lodge. I was mistakenly credited with saving his life. I was actually the driver of the snowcat."

MACONE PHOTO

O'Connor, who brought the idea of wall-to-wall machine grooming to Timberline in the mid-1960s.

"I first came down to Hood with my high school physics partner, Bud Valian," says O'Connor.

When he took over the ski school, he realized the need for a beginner area and helped develop the Phlox Point Road, a route for beginners to the bottom of Pucci lift. He initiated a "Ski School Practice Chair" a simulator for learning to load on a chairlift.

"There's no flat on that mountain so

Winter Sports Togs

Skiers picked up their imported Northland and Lund skis from Meier & Frank, Lipman Wolfe, the Portland Outdoor Store or the Beebe Company, headquarters for snowshoes, toboggans and ski equipment.

Homegrown parkas and pants came from Hirsch-Weis, America's first ski clothing manufacturer.

"Harold Hirsch's idea was that in the U.S., we needed affordable, durable, good-looking ski clothes," says his widow, Elizabeth. "His father owned Hirsch-Weis and made tents and sleeping bags. He also made jackets and pants that were dipped in paraffin, tin pants, for woodsmen.

"Harold thought the times were right because there were no ski clothes in America. People skied in whatever they, had but their clothes didn't keep out snow or cold. In 1931, Harold borrowed $1,500, a few sewing machines and in a corner of Hirsch-Weis, he designed and sewed ski clothes. His father thought he was crazy, but being an indulgent father, he gave in and let the boy go ahead.

"Harold was a skier and had a sense of design. He was putting out a line of ski clothing when he talked to Emilio Pucci. Emilio was an economics student at Reed College when Harold enlisted him to design ski clothes."

On the banks of the Willamette River, Hirsch and Pucci worked successfully. When WWII broke out, Pucci returned to his native Italy, and became a war hero.

Meanwhile, Hirsch had branched out, translated the name of his father's company to White Stag, and produced winter sports togs for nearly a half century.

Pucci became a famous fashion designer, best known for his bold and colorful "palazzo pajama" pants. Pucci's first fashion recognition was a chance encounter in Switzerland with a fashion photographer who saw Pucci in a ski suit of his own design. Both a ski run and chairlift bear his name at Timberline.

For years, White Stag held fashion shoots at Timberline using the lodge and the mountain as backdrop.

White Stag was sold in the 1980s, but the clothier's famous neon stag continues to gallop across Portland's skyline on the old Hirsch-Weis building.

During the Great Depression, a young Portland skier, Harold Hirsch began designing ski clothes. His Hirsch-Weis Winter Sports Togs were so popular that he was able to branch off from his father's manufacturing company, forming his own White Stag company.

ELVRUM COLLECTION

LEUTHOLD COLLECTION

Emilio Pucci di Barsento

FRIENDS OF TIMBERLINE COLLECTION

Emilio Pucci with a fashion model at Timberline Lodge. "Pucci coached the Reed College ski team in 1936-37," recalls team alumnus Neil Farnham. "Pucci designed our ski team sweater — his first attempt at ski clothing. White Stag then made sweaters with our mascot, the griffin, on the front."

Several private ski schools utilized Mt. Hood's slopes. "Camaraderie brought instructors together for an afternoon ritual of a few shared runs," says Vicki Hoefling Andersen. She taught skiing for the Jaycees and became one of the youngest certified ski instructors at age 16.

Teaching beginners summer 1958.

no place to learn to stop with just gravity," says O'Connor. "The nice thing about Pucci was that we could go down in a magic land. There'd be a storm whirling above Timberline, and we'd ski down in a magic zone below the storm."

O'Connor taught the Canadian Ski Instructors' Alliance technique and later wrote the ski manual *The Canadian Ski Technique*. He saw value in uniforms for his staff, so Timberline's instructors wore matching blue sweaters. Their customers often wore the latest in ski fashion, the wet look.

The other half of that Canadian import, Bud Valian, taught skiing, and became a well-known tinkerer in Government Camp. He built a mechanized ski-tuning machine, tried fiberglassing leather boots for stiffness, and raced down Timberline Road in a wheelchair.

"He had two broken legs at the time," says his wife Betsy Valian. "The USFS didn't take out all the Skiway towers. He was skiing down and hit a stanchion between towers full tilt. It practically took off his legs!"

In the 1950s, morphine was kept at the post office. The person sent to give him morphine was so shaken that he squirted out the opiate.

"A doctor pieced every bone back together," Valian adds. "When he broke his legs, ski instructors passed the hat. That's ski insurance in the ski business."

Bud Valian ran the Multorpor Ski School and owns a ski shop in Government Camp renowned for fine-tuning racers' skis.

An immense growth in the number of skiers fostered numerous schools on the mountain. Clubs organized lesson programs including the Jaycees, Mt. Hood Ski School, Powder Hounds and Western Ski Pros. Weekend ski schools filled Summit, Ski Bowl and Timberline.

"I convinced the Jaycees to move their ski school up to Timberline in 1966," says Portlander John Carson. "I was co-director at the time. We probably had 2,200 students up there at a time. We moved a lot of people with 50 buses up from town."

"I had a student who was like many students, uncoordinated," recalls John Hoefling who taught or ran several ski schools. "That's all right. I wasn't too coordinated either. At the end of three weeks, his mom said, 'My son is so

Flying Outriggers

In 1968, I put on the first Inner Ski conference in the U.S. with top instructors from around the world. I took a team of amputee skiers from Mt. Hood, borrowed a few from Denver, and we put on the first amputee skier demonstration in the world.

— LEE PERRY

Something touched Lee Perry's heart in 1960. He saw Warren Miller's movie which included a few frames of an amputee skier in Europe. By 1961, he convinced the Portland Junior Chamber to organize America's first Amputee Ski School.

"I knew that amputees had skied before," says Perry, not an amputee himself. "The word was out that if the amputee had not been a skier before the accident that made him an amputee, then he wouldn't become one. But I would not accept that. I went to work."

Perry borrowed outriggers — ski poles with small skis instead of tips — from amputee Dick Martin, a car racer and "a marvelous, gutsy skier." Martin became the first certified amputee ski instructor in the U.S.

Perry arm-twisted Jaycees Keith Carlson, Paul Nagel, Pat McPhail, Leo Olson, John Hoefling and Bob Howland to help acquire equipment, instructors and funds.

With $300 budgeted from the Jaycees, they acquired $1,500 in equipment from local shops donating mismatched skis, and two boxes full of non-matching after-ski boots.

They took Martin's outriggers and redesigned them to fit youngsters. Volunteers at a Portland machine shop donated work on new outriggers.

"Then I knocked on doors," says Perry. "The parents of the kids with amputations had the guts to let me take their child to the slopes. I asked those kids to do things that I should have been put in jail for. Not one kid ever quit."

Each winter weekend, Perry packed a carload of kids to Timberline, gave them ski equipment and outriggers and with the help of volunteer instructors, taught them to ski.

Aside from the challenge to learn to ski with one leg while using outriggers, the youngsters also mastered the rope tow, holding the rope with one hand and the two outriggers with the other.

"The first outriggers we made kept breaking," says Perry. "We'd go home every week and spend two nights fixing the outriggers."

By 1965, Perry and the Portland Jaycees published the *Amputee Ski Technique* manual.

Timberline hosted the fourth annual International Amputee Championship Slalom races in 1967. Olympian Gretchen Fraser distributed the trophies and became the first honorary member of the new Flying Outriggers Ski Club.

As amputees say, one must have a little humor to endure the challenges of skiing as Cal Andrews found out. He bought a pair of stylish Bogners in 1964, and asked his mother to tailor fit the stretch pants. She did but cut the wrong leg off!

"We kidded him so," laughs Perry. "We told him that the only way to get us off your back is to give the pants to another amputee with the same waist size, different leg. And he did!"

Currently the Adaptive Skiing Program at Timberline serves a variety of people with disabilities. Besides outriggers, the program uses a mono-ski which is a ski with a bucket mounted on it for the skier to sit in, a "sit-ski" sled, a "bi-ski" high performance mono-ski using two skis, and other tools to make the experience positive.

"The adaptive ski program and special equipment level the playing field for disabled people," says Trina Schoenberg, Timberline's Adaptive Program Coordinator. "Someone who can't climb the stairs can fly down the mountain."

Bud Nash directed the
Jaycee's Ski School and
later Timberline's Ski
School.

FRIENDS OF TIMBERLINE COLLECTION

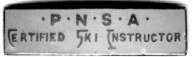

happy to do skiing because that's the
first activity he's ever been able to do.'
They hadn't told me that he had cere-
bral palsy, and I'm glad they hadn't. That
made it all worthwhile."

The 1960s' era of social change in
America saw an equipment and technique revolution as well. The radically
different metal Head skis sold for $100
a pair. Popular were Dickie Turtles, Ko-
mbi glove protectors for rope-tow
riding, knee-high gaiters and moon
boots. Ski boots evolved from leather
and lace-ups to plastic boots with metal
buckles.

A new teaching movement, the Professional Ski Instructors of America,
formed in 1961 to teach not European
style but American ski techniques.

Pacific Northwest Ski Instructors
Association recruited more than 750
instructors in the region and encouraged instructors to enroll in the annual
ski symposium, "a graduate school for
ski instructors." Ski instructors became certified professionals.

By the time the streaking fad
stormed the nation, Bud Nash managed the Timberline Ski School with
a flair for priceless fun.

"We had this monkey, and
who ever screwed up on the
slopes got the monkey," recalls
instructor Dick Collins. "If you

VIDONI COLLECTION

Vidoni + Nash - Thunderhead, 1961

Thunderhead Lodge housed the Jaycee Ski
School in 1961. "Bud Nash and I ran the Jaycee
Ski School together when he became chief
instructor at Timberline," says Jack Vidoni. "We
had a camaraderie about it. We'd have 108 buses
up there on a Saturday, a thousand people in
lessons at Summit Ski Area."

crashed in front of somebody, you were
fined 25 cents. If late to a meeting, it
cost 25 cents too. A big crash cost a
dollar. The money went into a party
fund. We had our party in the old Ski
Deli. We had six kegs of beer. We ended
up throwing Bud Nash in the pool.

Somebody pushed me in too. I had my neat ski sweater on and it turned a new color."

Also fading was the Graduated Length Method of teaching in which novices started on very short skis and graduated to longer skis as their skiing improved. Clothing brightened to day-glow in the 1980s, then faded again.

For a decade, Jonathan Lohnes and his Timberline Ski School staff focused on "teaching the individual rather than teaching skiing," he says. "It was quite different from the Europeans' approach to teaching. We emphasized edging skills, weight shift and rotary or turning skills. It was quite effective. The American Teaching Method became the model for teaching in the world."

His first year at Timberline was the lodge's 50th anniversary. White Stag outfitted the staff with anorak pullover jackets and blousy pants, a retro-style from the 1930s. Skis also went retro, growing longer. The 1990s saw super side cuts, fat boys and shaped skis. Through it all, teaching methodology remained rooted in the

Austrian basics of the stem turn.

"The Professional Ski Instructors of America use the American Teaching System," says Stuart Collins, Timberline Ski School Director. "One aspect is the service model which is relatively newly recognized as instruction that imparts upon the student how to have a better overall mountain experience."

PROFESSIONAL
SKI INSTRUCTOR
OF AMERICA

MT. KOHNSTAMM

KOHNSTAMM COLLECTION

O'CONNOR COLLECTION

Dick Collins — The Consummate Instructor

He's taught skiing for three decades, and more recently snowboarding on Mt. Hood. Nationally he is known as the old guy in the Polartec advertisement. He's on a snowboard with his patent grin and the caption reads, "Three wars. Three IRS audits. Three kidney stones. Anything but the cold."

He's Dick Collins, the consummate instructor who never had a bad ski lesson.

"Dick has a passion for sharing the good ski experience with everyone," says Stuart Collins, Timberline Ski School Director. "He took it upon himself to integrate his passion into his students' passion, a level of instruction that most instructors never attain."

He saw ski school directors come and go including Bud Nash, Doug Kinney, Bob Hinkle, Jeff Lokting, Jonathan Lohnes and Stuart Collins. Most exciting for Dick Collins is the advent of snowboarding.

"Most of snowboarding relates to skiing," says Collins. "I wanted to make it safer. That's why I got into snowboarding. People were running into people all over the hill. It became a big mess"

He started boarding a decade ago.

"I'd go out and cream myself like the rest of 'em," he laughs.

His hearing, not what it used to be, caused some confusion when a woman asked him for the powder room. He heard "powder run."

"Dick tells her to go down Victoria ski runs, and if there's no powder there, go up near Silcox Hut," laughs his wife, Liz. "He tells her, 'It's snowing so hard they'll never see your tracks!'"

Three wars.
Three IRS audits.
Three kidney stones.

Anything but the cold.

USED BY PERMISSION FROM POLARTEC

This Polartec advertisement ran in national magazines in 1997-98.

"Teaching is basically the same now as it was in the '70s when I started, but we have many new approaches to get a person to do something," says Dick Collins. "It makes it easy. In skiing, things change so much. For instance depending on the length of a shaped ski, it will carve a 10-foot arc or 30-foot arc. These things I'm still learning."

Nordically Speaking

From the earliest ski competitions in both Europe and the Pacific Northwest, Nordic or cross-country ski racing figured into the ski equation.

In 1931, the Pacific Northwestern Championships, sponsored by Cascade Ski Club, offered a cross-country race. Andy Roch of the Cascade Ski Club garnered class "B" in 50.30 minutes. Results do not list course distance.

A week later, the Hood River Ski Tournament included a five-mile race, won by Hjalmar Hvam in 30.03 minutes. Skyliners of Bend pitted racers against a 25-mile ski course.

Although Mt. Hood never developed into a highly-recognized cross-country venue, the West's first x-c ski school evolved at its base.

Klindt Vielbig organized the first Nordic ski school in 1967 after skiing and climbing Northwest peaks.

"I started x-c skiing for the adventure and to expand my winter recreation," says Vielbig who managed the Cloud Cap Chalet sports store at the time. "As x-c skis became available, and with direct imports from Norway, I was the first retail store in Oregon to sell x-c equipment."

Customers asked abut the waxing and techniques so it was logical for Vielbig to offer weekend lessons in his Nordic Ski School.

"Waxing was a real ordeal," he recalls before the advent of waxless skis. "As the students did not have the experience to wax properly, the instructors had to do most of it and supervise students' waxing. Finally, we bought a large portable propane tank and blow torch to speed up waxing."

The downside of waxing includes some particularly gooy purple klister for warm snow. During a lesson, one of Veilbig's students laboriously skied up to the class.

"She struggled along the track," recalls Vielbig. "I suddenly noticed there appeared to be a dark shadow flopping along under her right ski, a dark rag or cloth that I finally identified as my own prized Odlo jacket! She had carelessly left the track, wandered over my jacket and the klister glued it to her ski."

If the klister mark never left the navy-blue nylon, neither did Vielbig's mark on Nordic skiing. Vielbig went on to write the guidebook, *Cross-Country Ski Routes – Oregon*.

Meanwhile, Shelley Butler began teaching Nordic skiing in 1971.

ARTHUR PHOTO

Phil Hetz and Mary McLaren DeVore telemark between their shifts at the Cascade Dining Room, 1986. "That's the reason we worked," says Betsy Perrodin. "To ski!"

"Cross-country boomed in the mid-seventies," says Butler. "At Multorpor in 1978-83, we had 20 instructors on weekends and 15 classes." She operates Wy'east Nordic, teaching cross-country skiing and telemarking — a return to skiing's early roots.

He admits that for a time, instruction became so technique oriented that recreational skiers lost interest in ski schools.

"People needed to be precise at their work," says Collins. "They did not want to be precise at their fun. The pendulum swings now toward snowboarding. It's free form. Ski area managers played right into that. We used to have runs buffed to pool tables on a slant. Boring! Now (with snowboarding) we have holes and jumps, and the shift is back to fun."

While ski areas nationwide experience little growth in ski business, snowboarding revitalizes snowsports. Nationally, about 35 percent of lessons are for snowboarders. The Pacific Northwest leads the nation in percent of snowboarding lessons. More than half of lessons at Timberline are snowboarding.

"Ten years ago, those teaching snowboarding were skiers on a single plank," says Collins. "They tried all the techno lingo. It failed miserably. Now it's young folks looking for a way to make a living at snowboarding. They have brought all this fun onto the mountain. Many of them don't

Ski School Reunion pin.
KOHNSTAMM COLLECTION

know how to ski. They are snowboarders."

Collins tells his ski instructors to learn to snowboard or learn a new profession because he expects 60 to 65 percent of lesson requests in the next decade will be for snowboarding.

As ski areas and clubs transform to encompass snowsports into their master plans, the foundations that Otto Lang brought to Mt. Hood and America remain crucial. "The principle behind the Arlberg style is still around today," says Lang. "When you teach children to ski, you use the snowplow and the snowplow turn. The French have a wonder homily for ski teaching. *Plus ça change, plus c'est la meme chose*, which means, the more it changes, the more it is the same."

"I can ski the Austrian, the French and the American ski techniques," says Howard Hermanson. "I've been through all the wars with that technique stuff but my favorite is the American technique with a quiet upper body. It happened because of better boots and skis. We used to have to work so hard to turn skis. Now you throw your eyebrows and you turn."

Half-price fun in 1976.

As the Bullwheel Turns

Opposite page: Employees lived in dorms in Timberline Lodge with women on one side of the hall, men on the other, "As if that could keep us apart!" says Carol Haugk.

Riding the bullwheel lacks the glamour of riding a spitting-mad rodeo bull but not the adrenalin rush. Novices who neglect to get off the chair at the top terminal ride around the bullwheel. Lift operators rescue them.

While ski instructors receive the tips, ski patrollers the thanks, and racers the glory, lift operators and outdoor crews are unsung heroes of the mountain.

"We were doing some logging down on a trail, and one guy bet another that he could walk the cable on Pucci between two towers, probably 40 feet apart," says Steve Haugk a 35-year employee of Timberline. "He climbed up, crossed the cable and climbed down. We each paid him $10 or something."

It wasn't a bet that forced Haugk to do the same one winter when a youngster mis-loaded a chair and slipped off the seat. The child's mother held him by his jacket but couldn't pull him up into the chair. He dangled 20 feet above the snow.

Night Repairs. "Seems like we'd just get something repaired and it'd rip out the next day," says Tina Donovan who drove grooming machines for both Timberline and Ski Bowl. "My first winter at Ski Bowl, we had older cats. The tracks were just held together with a series of splices. I'd spend 12 hours grooming and two hours splicing. We finally got a new set of tracks, and a guy took the cat out pulling the gang rollers behind him, on the maintenance road. At a hair-pin turn, the gang rollers stuck. He forced it and ripped up the brand new tracks."

Haugk shut off the lift, went hand over hand up the cable to the chair, climbed down and pulled the boy back into his mother's arms.

"I had to do something," was all Haugk said.

Like the massive ski lift bullwheels which keep the lift cable going around, the employees are the cogs that mobilize operations. They refer to their life and labor in soap-opera terms: As the Bullwheel Turns.

People ski across the lift crews' boots, poke them with ski poles and fall on top of them on the ramp. Undaunted by cruel weather — and visitors on rental gear — outdoor employees accept challenges as the Brussels sprouts of life's adventure potluck. Skiing is dessert.

MACONE PHOTO

"There were four of us in that first lift crew, fall of 1939," says Norm Wiener, a prominent Portland lawyer. "I was paid $60 a month with room and board."

An operations manual had not yet been thought of for chairlifts. No one knew how to load a chairlift in 1939. Lift operators initially stopped the machine for each skier to sit on the single-seater Magic Mile. This created a lengthy lift line and ride. After a few days, the crew decoded the secret of loading. They coaxed the skier, the chair and the lap blanket together without halting the lift.

"I was the only one in the crew who skied for recreational purposes. When we closed the lift each day, I had a mile ski run back to the lodge. One particular day, a whiteout set in. Heavy snow, and a driving wind caused visibility to be less than 50 feet. I snowplowed down directly under the cables of the lift. I knew that if I lost sight of the cables, I could well be lost. I made it — but rest assured that my knees were shaking long after I arrived at the lodge."

He recalls once when the engineer operating the lodge's power plant had an argument with the manager and cut the power. The sheriff came to quell the mutiny.

Others came to Timberline to strike up the band.

"The highlight of my years at Timberline were the summers I spent up on Hood's glaciers," says Walt Aeppli, a Swiss engineer whose "Edelweiss Irregulars" trio played in the Blue Ox bar. He stayed for 40 years as engineer.

Aeppli and his accordion-playing partner and yodeler performed during weddings, Golden Rose festivities and other events. Walt's Baby ski run is named for his daughter, and Aeppli's Corner is named for his Studebaker convertible.

"A rock crusher sat on a corner of Timberline Road while it was being built in 1948," he recalls. "I tried to drive around it and got too far over. That was the end of the Studebaker. I landed on my head — that saved me!"

Aeppli retired from Timberline in 1987, "but the building kept me here. I'm semi-retired now."

Instead of retiring after work, employees tumbled outdoors to ski.

"I fit rental skis in the ski shop all day, mounted bindings and tuned skis," recalls Norm Dversdal of the mid 1940s. "One evening when I got off shift, a few of us built a ski jump behind the lodge. People could see us out the back windows. We spent several hours in the fresh snow, packing the slope, hiking sideways, packing out the run and making the jump at the bottom."

"The Blue Ox rocked back then," recalls **Gary Hohnstein. "I was dancing one time with Lucy Haynes. As my version of the story goes, I was dancing on a table with Lucy, and she hit me on the head with a bottle and split my head open. Everybody else's version said that I hit my head on a sprinkler. Somebody saw a little blood coming out from under my baseball hat. I took my hat off and there was a big gush of blood. Six stitches!"**

Dversdal says he wasn't much of a jumper but decided to hike higher for a bigger jump.

"It was snowing hard and it was difficult to see," he says. "I overshot the landing and couldn't turn because I landed in soft snow, not what we had boot packed. I hit the lodge and went partially through a window! I backed up and looked through the broken window to apologize. I saw that my ski-shop boss was inside."

"When I came to the U.S., I had only $38 in my pocket," recalls Austrian instructor and coach Erich Sailer. **"They gave me a room in the lodge where the windows didn't close. I woke up in the morning and I was covered with snow. We had nothing — no radio, tv or car. All it was was teaching and shoveling customers' cars out. And shuffleboard. There was no social life except a once-a-week cocktail party in the Blue Ox where we went with customers for a little socializing."**

BLUE OX PIN: ARTHUR COLLECTION

"Several of us went up for spring skiing," recalls Pattie Wessinger. "We'd ride a cat up at 5:30 a.m. and ski until 1:00."

"In May, the skiing was lovely," recalls Bill Wessinger. "We would start in the east and as the sun softened the snow, we'd move west. We ate lunch below the Hogsback at about the 10,000-foot elevation, Camp 10."

Fearing that they would lose their jobs, the teenagers scrambled to the trail down the mountain.

"I don't know if my boss recognized me or not. We skied to Government Camp and became blameless, we thought, because we were in Govy 'all evening' and couldn't get up the snowed-in, closed road."

Because of the road and limited housing, outdoor crews bunked on Timberline Lodge's ground floor while indoor employees occupied the third floor. Gals roomed on one side of the hall, guys on the other, "As if that would

keep us apart!" laughs Carol Belbusti Haugk who worked at Timberline for three decades.

Spring thaws and highway rotary plows opened the scenic Highway 35 for summer tourists.

"We came to Timberline in 1959," she says. "Four of us, Adrienne Shields, Jill Schilling, Alice Miles and I drove across the country from New England, going to jobs in California. We stayed overnight in The Dalles, saw Hood and went crazy. We had our skis. The waitress told us that Highway 35 just opened. We saw on a map, 'Government Camp.' There must be an army base there! That's where we are staying.

"Of course when we got to Government Camp, there was just a maintenance shed, so up to Timberline we went. A room, a dorm Chalet for four was $12. Excuse me? That's too expensive.

"The four of us went to the cafeteria to decide what we'd do. John West or Hal Martin said he was going up to set race flags for Canadian Weekend. Did any of us want to ski? So we went up and skied. When we came back, we had jobs."

Haugk joined the staff and eventually managed the ski shop.

"We had fun parties, pajama parties for employees that lasted all night," says Gary Hohnstein. He worked in the

MACONE PHOTO

rental shop in 1963. "It was the Breakfast Club. We'd go swimming, play all night then at 6 a.m. have breakfast in the Barlow Room which used to be the cafeteria. I'd play the cook. I flipped pancakes over my shoulder, and people had to catch 'em. Pancakes would be hanging from the light fixtures."

Breakfast Club meetings started after midnight, "so we had to sleep whenever we could," adds Haugk.

As customers demanded more lodging, employee quarters were converted to guest rooms. The failed Skiway's lower terminal, Thunderhead Lodge, housed employees instead of the Skiway. Thunderhead hosted the fun from 1964 through the late 1970s.

"My wife and I were strict managers," recalls Red Hower. "We had inspections every Saturday. Of course there were a few dinkleheads that you'd want to drop kick out the door, but most employees

living in Thunderhead were very neat and clean."

Others lived in tiny villages of Zigzag, Rhododendron, Welches, Brightwood and Parkdale.

"I spent the winter of 1971 in a little tumbledown cabin beside the Zigzag River," says former ski instructor Michael Elcock. "Road 38 was choked with drifts until late March, so I had to hike in almost half a mile. There was no central heating, in fact no heating of any kind except for a big open fireplace. Until I managed to scrounge a truckload of teak ends from an old carpenter, it was cold in there. As it was, the fire never stayed on all night, and there was usually frost on the floor in the mornings."

Timberline provided transportation up the mountain in an old red school bus, the Crummy.

"One morning people sat in the bus wondering where the driver was," recalls Artie Speicher, outdoor maintenance at Timberline in the 1970s and 80s. "There's one minute before the bus was to leave and no driver. Out of the back of the bus came the sound

HOHNSTEIN COLLECTION

Gary Hohnstein worked several positions at Timberline beginning in 1963. The lift crew knew him on the slopes because he skied in pink gaiters.

.05¢

.05¢

.05

.10

.25

Timberline Lodge

N⁰ 12095

MEAL TICKET BOOK

$20.00

Signature

Good Only for Lodge Employees

HARRINGTON COLLECTION

Timberline Lodge employee meal ticket book.

Dine and Dash

The guest was a trouble maker from the start, an oddball, said the staff. When asked about the bill for his week's stay, he wouldn't pay up. Finally assistant manager Joe Baudoin confronted the obstinate guest.

"Baudoin went in the room and found that the guy was gone," recalls Kohnstamm. "The hotel-room window was open, and he'd jumped out and skied to Government Camp. He had two suitcases and didn't use poles."

As it does at Mt. Hood, snow fell so hard that the dine-and-dasher wallowed in the flats of the Glade Trail.

"We sent a Sno-Cat after him," says Kohnstamm. "He was so relieved to be caught that he paid up."

of an alarm clock. Up pops bus driver Dave Craig. He walks to the front and then starts the bus. It seems that he had too much fun the night before at Charlie's Mountain View and wanted to make sure that he was on time for work."

Employees were not the only passengers.

"Sam Berger used to ride the bus up to the lodge in the mornings," recalls former lift crew and ticket seller Jackie Wettleson. "Sam, a dog, weighed 40 pounds. He was low to the ground, brown with black markings, a buck jaw, crooked teeth and he sometimes grinned at you. He would ride up the chairlift by himself too, sitting on the Magic Mile looking for who knows what."

His owner, Larry Berger says that Sam's teeth finally began rotting out from all the maple bars.

"Sam knew the Trailways bus schedule," says Berger. "He'd stand there looking sad as travelers got off the bus. He'd get people to give him Huckleberry Inn's maple bars."

If getting to work didn't discourage people to move to fairer climes, the work itself might. Complaining guests could disillusion the most affable of employees. Bob Webb, sports writer for the *Oregonian*, wrote

Ski fashion hat from the 1970s in the Ski Horse located in the basement of The Clothes Horse on Broadway and Morrison in Portland.

about the 1939 national races.

"Funniest of the series of laughable incidents that marked the national ski tournament week at Timberline Lodge was the result of a fundamental difference in the European and American hotel setups.

"It seems that the Swiss women's team and several other continental entrants left their shoes and boots outside their doors on retiring, expecting them to be cleaned and greased.

"The next morning there sat the foot gear, cold and untouched.

"Manager Arthur Allen had a tough

time pacifying the irritated shoe-leav-ers and explaining that boot-greasing and shoe-shining weren't part of Tim-berline's service."

Serving new skiers and old, the ski rental shop is often a customer's first contact with skiing. Employees spent hours drying out leather rental boots, replacing edges on wooden skis and treating bases with Toko wax.

"I made $1.65 an hour," recalls Hohn-stein. "I could sell skis, but what I could really sell were tight ski pants. I could convince the gals that the pants weren't tight enough. They'd try on Bogners or Heads or White Stags. I'd tell them they needed a smaller size. They loved me."

In those days, mountain people sometimes looked down, literally and figuratively, upon novices in tight pants.

"We treated the flatlanders with dis-dain," recalls Elcock. "They were the people who flocked up to the moun-tains on weekends, decked out in fancy designer ski-wear. They had all the ski gear, expensive boots and skis and shiny 'wet-look' clothing.

"We on the other hand, skied in blue jeans and hand-me-downs and anything we could purloin or persuade from the manufacturers' reps. But we could ski. The flatlanders looked good, but few of them were in the same league as us when they had skis on. We were young and probably a bit arrogant. But we were all broke, so we didn't have much else except a rather misplaced pride in what we could do."

Jim Coffel became skiing's pied piper by offering van rides from Portland to Hood for over a decade.

Pride for the maintenance crew is buried under thick ice. They chisel the coating of ice off lift cables, chairs and bullwheels. They call themselves ice busters.

Ice busters spend slippery hours in howling winds, dangling from towers to clear the lift system.

"Over the years I have pounded a lot of ice off of lift equipment," says Artie Speicher. "In the East, it is man-made ice from snowmaking, but at Timber-line, mother nature does the best job. Over all of the years of using hammers,

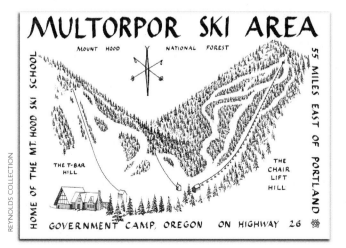

MULTORPOR SKI AREA

MOUNT HOOD   NATIONAL FOREST

55 MILES EAST OF PORTLAND

HOME OF THE MT. HOOD SKI SCHOOL

THE T-BAR HILL

THE CHAIR LIFT HILL

GOVERNMENT CAMP, OREGON   ON HIGHWAY 26

I never saw anyone get as attached to his hammer as Larry Labby. He even named his hammer 'Lucille' in honor of B.B. King's guitar, Lucille. We were on tower 21 beating the ice build up when Lucille slipped from a guy's grasp and fell into the tower."

"It was my day off," recalls Labby. "Somebody had borrowed my hammer. When I came in to work, Artie had bad news for me. They'd lost Lucille, just a Sears Roebuck hammer, really."

"I thought that Larry was going to cry," laughs Speicher. "We went back

Rime frost coats the top station of the Magic Mile double chairlift after an extreme storm.

and had a ceremony for Lucille. Lucille rests in that tower to this day, an icon to ice busters."

An institution of the Magic Mile double chairlift, "Big Chris" Carl Christianson, spent more than a decade on lift crew, mostly at the remote outpost of midway on the Mile. Since he didn't ski, somebody gave him a sitski.

"It looked like a bicycle," recalls Jamie Priestley who worked lift crew in 1980. "It had a front fork, bicycle handle bars and one big ski under the seat with another short ski under the handlebars for steering."

Big Chris buckled small skis to each work boot and rode the sitski down to the maintenance shop after every shift — and after he'd barked "Midway clear!" into the phone.

"I hooked up with Big Chris to make sure he got down on the sitski," says Priestley. "He made a big sweeping turn near the top of Pucci. Suddenly it looked like a cowboy had lassoed him off the top of his sitski. He hit a rope strung across the top of Pucci's runs. Hit it with his neck. Turned out he was okay, just a little hoarse for a few days."

The last lift crew on top of the Mile skied or walked down to clock out. One late afternoon, Hohnstein, who became lift crew supervisor, called the top operator, Jackie Wettleson.

A Thousand Words

Photographers and other artists indelibly inked the image of Timberline and Mt. Hood into the world's eye. Ray Atkeson, Hugh Ackroyd, Hal Lidell, Al Monner, Jim Vincent, Dick Powers and other photographers created a public enchantment with Mt. Hood through dramatic photography.

Atkeson roamed west from Kansas as a teenager, picked fruit in Hood River and by 1927, moved to Portland. By 1929, he apprenticed at PhotoArt Commercial Studio where he worked until 1946 when he launched a freelance career. Until his death stopped his shutter in 1990, Atkeson's photos graced magazine covers and filled books. He accumulated 75,000 images and was recognized by Oregon Governor Neil Goldschmidt as Oregon's Photographer Laureate in 1987.

"In the 1930s his black-and-white photographs were printed in the rotogravure sections of the nation's leading newspapers, giving people their first glimpse of the mountains and ski country of Oregon," says Atkeson's stepson, Rick Schafer. "Over the next 50 years, he was a pioneer in the acceptance of outdoor photography as an art form.

He set a standard for the style and character of color landscape photography."

Atkeson's friend and fellow commercial photographer, Hugh Ackroyd, focused on fashion, aerials, industrial locations and the occasional mountain fatality. Upon a

Hugh Ackroyd and camera.

$500 bet, he once convinced a professional model to ride the single-seater Magic Mile lift wearing only ski boots and Northland skis.

"We had a great capacity for fun," says Ackroyd.

For 30 years Dick Powers has been the official photographer for Mt. Hood Meadows. He photographed the stormy opening day, Jan. 28, 1968. At one time 125 of his photographic images adorned the walls of Meadow's base lodge. He calls himself a mercenary with cameras.

"I bill myself as a pseudo employee," laughs Powers. "I get the perks, I wear the Meadows' coat and freeload on a season pass, but I've never been on the payroll!"

Ray Atkeson often skied with 30 pounds of camera equipment in his rucksack. ATKESON COLLECTION

"I'd been working for Edna Kruse at Huckleberry Inn serving breakfast to drunks after the bar closed," recalls Linda Reid. **"Edna introduced me to Dave Butt. He hired me to work lift crew on the all-girl lift crew."**

"I said I'd come get her with the snow cat because there was a bad blizzard," he recalls. "All of a sudden I couldn't tell where I was going. I had run right into the 20-foot-high back berm of Palmer's lower terminal. I radioed Jackie to tell her to walk over to Palmer. I wait and wait. No Jackie. I call again and no answer. So I plan to walk around the berm to see if I can see her. I get out of the cat and kaboom! She lands right on top of me. I don't know how she didn't break my neck."

"I walked right off the bank," says Wettleson. "It was a total white out, couldn't see a thing. Gary broke my fall."

Wettleson was part of the all-girl lift crew hired by Dave Butt in 1978.

"That was the easiest season we had," recalls Hohnstein. "They showed up and did their work. No moaning and groaning. You send them out to shovel and guys complain but girls just do it."

"I figured hiring an all-girl lift crew provided opportunity for them to do something other than waitressing," says Butt. "They dealt with the public a lot better than the guys."

"Here was this Jerry Garcia-looking guy, Dave Butt, who taught us how to run the lift and treated us well," recalls Linda Reid. "There were about ten of us, Baby Kay Johnson, Marlene Peoples, Jackie Wettleson and her friend Kim

Lindell, the Pfeiffer sisters, Becky Talsma, and later Brenda Parton, Jean Arthur and Genean Kleinbach."

They spruced up lift shacks, baked goodies for Big Chris, and charmed the guests.

"If you were a gal, you got hired," says Marlene Peoples who later joined the ski patrol. "There were hard times and good times working on the mountain. One winter we got snowed in, February 1980. Nobody could get up the road. I was the only patroller on the mountain. It snowed so hard that the groomer, Jeff Flood, could groom only one run. By the time he made one circle, it was snowed in again."

They cooked up schemes to keep each other laughing. They decorated the shop Christmas tree with jumper cables instead of popcorn strings. They tested each other's mettle.

"Over the years we pulled many pranks," says Speicher. "I remember the time a grease zerk fitting was glued onto Steve Haugk's toolbox. Then a bead of grease was laid down on the rim of the box and the cover was closed so that it looked like someone pumped it full of grease. (Haugk always said that if there was a grease fitting on a tree, someone would grease it.) The final touch was to put a dab of grease on the fitting so it looked authentic.

"No one could get up or down the road," recalls Lift Crew Superviosor, Becky Talsma. "The employees stayed in the lodge and worked long days just to keep everything operating. We had to flag cars in the parking lot with bamboo sticks so that when the highway department finally did make it up the road four days later, they wouldn't hit the cars buried in the parking lot."

Skiing the Parking Lot

The ski shop has long been the hang out for technology lovers.

"When I first started working in the rental shop, it was in Timberline Lodge next to the ski shop," recalls Skosh Peoples. "On a busy Saturday, we'd rent 800 pairs of skis."

Brothers Dave and Phil Hetz made this "skiing-off-the-roof" photograph. Dave Hetz, formerly a bartender at Timberline, actually skis on the snow berm made of snow cleared from the parking lot. Phil, a Timberline waiter, positioned himself on Pucci ski run to capture the trick, circa 1995.

HETZ PHOTO

The customer line wove down the hall, through the foyer and sometimes out the front doors. He and Duane "Auggie" Augustine spent three minutes per skier, outfitting, adjusting and collecting money.

"If they came in with their boots on the wrong feet, we'd just let 'em go," laughs Peoples. "If they rented equipment and put boots on the wrong feet, we'd discreetly tell them, 'You come in looking like Daffy Duck!' All the renters skied through the parking lot, though. I don't know why, but they did."

Smelly wool socks and soaked rental boots would get the rental shop crew thinking of new ways to ski. Bill Duffy bolted old skis together. Instead of bindings, screwheads poked above the surface, so the rider stood on the double wide plank like he rode a surfboard.

"You stood one foot in front of the other standing on screws that were partially into the skis for traction," recalls Artie Speichter. "You rode until the inevitable happened which was a fall of unusually spectacular acrobatics."

"We'd see everything up here," says Peoples. "One time the army brought up a breakaway ski. You'd fold it in half and screw it together to go in a pack."

Although Duffy's ski didn't become a commercial success, ski testing did. It began with K2 skis about 1980. Testing product materials rather than performance, ski patrollers and other employees carved in the abrasive snow.

"Summer skiing was to our advantage," says Peoples. "We'd get icy mornings and slushy afternoons. K2 saw us and said, 'This is a goldmine.' They tested product materials, different glues, rubbers and parts to make a better ski."

"Now we build a ski on Monday, Tuesday and Wednesday, then drive down to Timberline and test it the rest of the week," says Stu Remple from Washington-based K2 and Olin skis. "We get in 350 skier days with over 200 prototype skis on 50 different skiers. We get in 35,000 Palmer runs, where May through September the snow and services are consistent for testing."

Despite today's high-tech and high-priced skis and snowboards available, a posted sign near the parking lot reads: "Please do not ski in parking lot."

"The next morning Haugk did a double take. It did look like the toolbox was full of grease. He later got even with me by filling my ratchet sockets with chili at the chili cook-off. I had to chisel the chili out of the sockets. Some of the ratchet sockets still have chili on them!"

The outdoor crews did not exclude the public from their pranks.

"We had the Barker twins, handsome young men on the lift crew," recalls John Macone, public relations manager for Timberline in the 1950s and 60s. "One of their main gags while working the Magic Mile chairlift was to catch the attention of some tourist and say, 'I'll see you at the top.' When the person would reach Silcox Hut, the other twin ran around the hut, all out of breath. He'd say, 'We're a little shorthanded today.'"

Birth announcements for twins, John and Jeffrey, also announced Timberline's new double-seater Magic Mile lift.

Of all the toil, the hardships and the laughs, skiing with a pack of good friends tops the list.

"We absconded with a cat one day," admits Dave Butt. "We snuck over to Sand Canyon to ski. We had Big Chris with his sitski and took one of the Kohnstamm kids in case we got caught. We took Big Chris up to Illumination Rock. He'd never been there before. At sunset we skied down with Big Chris flying across the rocks and ripping the bases off his sitski. We had a good time."

At the end of a long day when temperatures are well below freezing, one last task awaits: shoveling out personal vehicles to drive home. Steve Haugk readied to do just that when skier Michael Dale of Oregon City walked in the shop. Dale's truck wouldn't start.

"As we walked out, my son looked up at Steve and asked, 'Aren't you going to bring your tool box?'" Dale wrote in the *Oregonian* in 1985.

"Steve looked at the child, reached into his parka's side pocket, and pulled out a medium size screwdriver.

Peter Thompson and Steve Haugk build Blossom Chairlift in 1981.

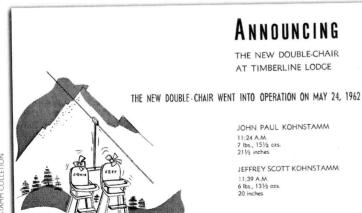

ANNOUNCING

THE NEW DOUBLE-CHAIR
AT TIMBERLINE LODGE

THE NEW DOUBLE-CHAIR WENT INTO OPERATION ON MAY 24, 1962

JOHN PAUL KOHNSTAMM
11:24 A.M.
7 lbs., 15½ ozs.
21½ inches

JEFFREY SCOTT KOHNSTAMM
11:39 A.M.
6 lbs., 13½ ozs.
20 inches

Escapade with the most lovable idiots

"I hung around with an ice skater, Clyde Cameron, back in 1939," says photographer Dick Powers. "His idea was to shovel the road open to get in to Frog Lake and ice skate.

"We started shoveling, side by side until dark. We got 300 yards. So I went back to fix some food. The next morning, I woke up and Clyde was no where around. I found him sitting at the lake. He decided it was not such a good thing to shovel to the lake — a half mile. So there was no ice skating afterall. It was an escapade with the most loveable idiots."

"'Chairlift repair kit, son,' he said with a confident smile. Using only his screwdriver, Steve had my truck running in 20 seconds."

Lift operators and the behind-the-scenes mechanics, groomers and others deserve credit for making skiing a joy. As the Bullwheel Turns is a tight brother and sisterhood of mountain dwellers who help one another. When lodge secretary Vida Lohnes needed to shovel out her car, somebody got the bucket loader. When fellow employee and long-time reservationist Mary Jane Valian became ill, they raised each other's spirits. When Big Chris earned a company-paid Hawaii vacation, they held the Govy Olympics. Big Chris needed a companion to travel through busy airpots, so they raised money to send his friend, Bob Butler, on the trip.

"We had a wood-splitting contest, a maplebar and coffee chugging contest and tobacco spitting contest," says Dave Butt. "What I remember most is the dog derby from the post office to the Village Store. A truck carried a fishing pole tied with dog bones, you know, because all Govy dogs chase cars. The race started fine until the bones fell off in front of Valian's Ski Shop. There was a big dog fight. Meanwhile some little fufu dog won."

Big Chris won too. His Hawaii vacation was the trip of a lifetime.

The lives and times in Government Camp include include ten-foot snow berms, long drives to school for kids

Timberline employees Mary Jane Valian, Jeanne Tucker, and Darrell & Lori Snowbarger, enjoy lunch on Timberline Lodge's veranda, circa 1985. "Employees used to eat together in the Ski Deli, but on nice days we'd sit in the sun together. On a clear day, you could see Mt. Jefferson and all the Cascades to the south. Mary Jane knew the names of all the mountains."

REID COLLECTION

and of course skiing.

"I tied little Swiss goat bells on to my children's shoes so we could hear them when they skied," recalls Marcel King who owned Battle Axe Inn with her husband and parents from 1929 to the late 1940s. "You skied or you didn't get around much in winter."

"I shoveled snow for a lift ticket on the old Mile," recalls John West of the 1950s. "But what I remember best was hanging out in Cascade Ski Club as a kid. We didn't know that we would get high on the lacquer the jumpers put on their skis. We'd be in there with the jumpers, college boys. They drank *Akvavit*, alcohol from potatoes. They would give us a nip. So we got to be their buddies."

Few children lived in Government Camp yet they played on a grand scale — after hot, fresh cinnamon doughnuts at Darr's Mountain Shop.

A sled hill began at Summit and ran through town. Kick-the-can started in Cascade Ski Club's parking lot and in-

O'CONNOR COLLECTION

BAT CAT

cluded the entire town. Capture-the-Flag incorporated a mountain top.

"When we were growing up in Govy, the kids had this internal war," recalls Shelley Butler. "We were friends, but some of us were better friends. Bruce Haynes and I had a flag, and we'd put it up on a pole on top Multorpor Mountain. You could see it from Govy. Other kids would see our flag, hike up and replace it with their own. Bruce and I would go up and put ours up again — it was just a sheet. It was fun and lasted several summers."

"You have to be a little crazy to live up here," says Lucy Haynes who moved to Government Camp from Portland in 1963. "For one thing, you have to like yourself here because you are alone a lot. A gal once asked me about the cultural advantages of living on the mountain. I answered, 'Two bars.'"

Despite roof-top deep snow in the winter and battalions of mosquitoes in summer, the mountain people stay because they love the climatic extremes, the physical challenges, and the bullwheel turning.

As Jon Tullis writes in his column, "Mountain Journal," for the *Sandy Profile*, "For nearly 12 months out of the year we pray for (snow), curse at it, drive through it, shovel it, measure it, move it, groom it, pile it up and push it around."

The bullwheel keeps turning.

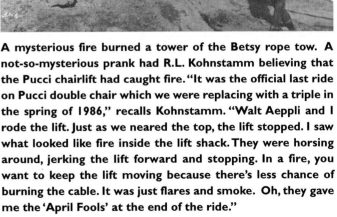

Skiers feel so strongly about the bullwheel that someone built a monument to it in Rhododendron.

A mysterious fire burned a tower of the Betsy rope tow. A not-so-mysterious prank had R.L. Kohnstamm believing that the Pucci chairlift had caught fire. "It was the official last ride on Pucci double chair which we were replacing with a triple in the spring of 1986," recalls Kohnstamm. "Walt Aeppli and I rode the lift. Just as we neared the top, the lift stopped. I saw what looked like fire inside the lift shack. They were horsing around, jerking the lift forward and stopping. In a fire, you want to keep the lift moving because there's less chance of burning the cable. It was just flares and smoke. Oh, they gave me the 'April Fools' at the end of the ride."

Passing the Torch — The Kohnstamm Family

"Dick Kohnstamm has done more for skiing and for Oregon than anyone alive," says former ski instructor John Hoefling. "He put Timberline on the map."

From his first days at Timberline, Kohnstamm's vision of a ski and hotel operation never wavered. The venture began as a blue highway that became a sleek parkway after four and a half decades.

When Kohnstamm stepped from Portland social worker to mountain hotelier in 1955, Timberline Lodge was a fire hazard and a bust. Some suggested that the magnificent structure be torn down. Instead Kohnstamm borrowed money, grabbed a broom and went to work.

"I thought it might take ten years to whip this place into shape," admits Kohnstamm. "It took 30. I had a tiger by the tail and couldn't let go. I owed so much money that I had to make Timberline successful just to pay the bills. I couldn't walk away although at the end of my second year, I thought about it. I was in real debt, and it didn't snow. Then a miraculous thing happened. A movie director wanted to film *All the Young Men*. Sydney Poitier, Alan Ladd and a whole studio booked the lodge. If not for that movie, I couldn't have made payroll. That saved me."

He realized that an occasional miracle couldn't keep the engine rooms running — good employees could. Many shared his passion about Timberline. What he learned from them he carries daily as his map light: Carol Haugk recruited high-energy employees; Steve Haugk trouble-shot with analytical genius; Jon Tullis counters confrontation with positive phraseology.

In the midst of business, Kohnstamm met and married Minnesotan Molly DeLong who came to Timberline on a summer junket between college and Europe. Their children, Kevin, Jeff, John, and David attended Portland schools and spent weekends on the mountain.

"We had room 112, next to our parents in room 110," recalls the youngest son, David. "When the snow was just right, we'd place a board between our window ledge and the snow outside, over the crevasse between the building and the snow and use it as a bridge. We'd ski right out our window."

Their dog, Toko, followed them as they skied then ran back up hill while the boys rode Pucci.

Aboard their red sleigh, a Tucker Sno-Cat, they bounded into the woods on the family's annual Christmas tree hunt.

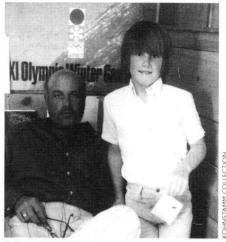

**R.L. and Jeff Kohnstamm
in the office circa 1970.**

"I believed in Santa Claus much later than my friends," laughs Kevin, the eldest. "I knew the department store Santas were frauds, but at Timberline, I saw the reindeer and the real Santa."

While the boys learned to ski from their certified ski instructor mother, they learned the ski business at the dining room table from their "certified *apres-ski* instructor" father.

"The Lodge was just a big house to us," Kevin adds.

CERTIFIED
APRES-SKI
INSTRUCTOR

That big house, Kohnstamm always believed, was the "people's place," and he was the innkeeper. After busy weekends, his kids could find him sweeping the lobby or shoveling doorways. Meanwhile, they had fun.

TIMBERLINE LODGE
GOVERNMENT CAMP, OREGON
WE GUARANTEE POSTAGE
DROP IN ANY MAIL BOX

"We'd build snow caves in front of the lodge and throw snowballs at people," laughs Kevin. "Or we'd get little rubber creatures and tie them to spools of thread and drop them slowly down from the balcony onto guests. If they got scared and we got scared, we'd drop the spool on guests' heads."

Their first jobs were at Timberline.

"When the twins Jeff and John worked up here, Steve Haugk used to give them the worst jobs possible," laughs Gary Hohnstein. "They had to clean the dipper stick box from the gear box at the top of Pucci. It's one of the worst jobs at a ski area. They did it, never complained. Steve used to holler at them, and they never said a word to their dad. Now Jeff's the boss. I told Haugk he's in for trouble now."

The transition from Richard Kohnstamm's family operation to his son Jeff's small corporation officially began in 1992 when Jeff moved into to his father's office. He packed a Cornell University degree in hotel management, restaurant experience in Switzerland and a knack for understanding the ski industry.

"My passion for Timberline is in maintaining the integrity of the historic place while staying in front of the challenges of a modern world," says Jeff.

Award plaques hang from the clear-pine office wall that father and son share: Snow Farmer of the Year; Community

RL and friends.

Service Award from Mt. Hood Chamber of Commerce; Governor's Award 1986; and National Trust of Historic Preservation Award. None carries more significance and exhilaration for Kohnstamm than his induction into the Ski Hall of Fame where he joins the Otto Langs and Dave McCoys (Mammoth Mountain) of the world.

"The high point for me was testifying before the U.S. Senate Interior Committee on the value of Timberline, and why we needed an appropriation to do the government expansion, the new wing, day lodge and a garage," he says of his 1972 trip to Washington D.C.

Yet in the back of his mind lurks the haunting image of his first day as manager of Timberline: the broken bullwheel in Silcox Hut, shredded drapery in the lodge and dust shadows where furnishings had been stolen. "That was my present from previous mismanagement."

His gifts to the people's place are many. He resurrected the lodge from sure demise. He established summer skiing. He accomplished what most others only dreamed.

While the senior Kohnstamm came to Timberline with the right combination of education and temperament to piece together the map of skiing for Oregon, for Jeff the passion is in the systemization of running a 20th century icon at a 21st century tempo.

"In this mechanized time, it's hard to fathom what my father started with at Timberline," says Kevin. "Now you see computerized lifts, state-of-the-art communications and hydrostatic groomers. He walked into that world of the 1950s and made it work."

Now Jeff's work focuses on employee teams managing computerized operations. His first-of-its-kind Palmer Express quad chairlift withstands weather no other machine dares. He communicates via the internet while his father resists computers and insists on using stamps, typewriters and a good old-fashioned telephone. Gone are the days when his phone number was simply "Timberline Toll-station-one." Here are the days when 32 phone lines reach Timberline and an address begins with "www."

Now semi-retired, Kohnstamm can still be found with a broom in hand, sweeping the lobby. He offers Jeff some advice. "You have to visualize where you're going and go there."